Collins

Starting a Business

Collins

HarperCollins Publishers
77-85 Fulham Palace Road
Hammersmith
London W6 8JB

First edition 2014

10 9 8 7 6 5 4 3 2 1

© HarperCollins Publishers 2014

ISBN 978-0-00-750718-4

Collins® is a registered trademark of HarperCollins Publishers Limited

www.collins.co.uk

A catalogue record for this book is available from the British Library

Typeset in India by Aptara

Printed and bound in Great Britain by Clays Ltd, St Ives plc

The Publisher and authors wish to thank the following rights holders for the use of copyright material: adapted text from *Learning Styles Helper's Guide* by Peter Honey and Alan Mumford (Pearson Education Ltd, 2009) reproduced by permission of Pearson Education.

Every effort has been made to contact the holders of copyright material, but if any have been inadvertently overlooked, the Publisher will be pleased to make the necessary arrangements at the first opportunity.

Illustrations by Scott Garrett

MIX
Paper from
responsible sources
FSC C007454

FSC™ is a non-profit international organisation established to promote the responsible management of the world's forests. Products carrying the FSC label are independently certified to assure consumers that they come from forests that are managed to meet the social, economic and ecological needs of present and future generations, and other controlled sources.

Find out more about HarperCollins and the environment at
www.harpercollins.co.uk/green

What kind of business will you run?

So, you know that you want to run your own business. You have a few ideas in mind that get you excited but how do you decide where to start?

Your passion, skills and experience

Take a good look at yourself. Is there something you're particularly passionate about? Have you always wondered whether you could turn your passion into a business? You may have a talent or skill which would enable you to start a business in a certain field, such as hairdressing or baking. Or you might be a professional, such as a lawyer, dentist or physiotherapist, and have realized that, rather than working for someone else, you now have the skills and experience to set up your own practice. Alternatively, you have identified a problem in your community that you think you might just have a solution for, or maybe you've come up with an idea that would make your life or the lives of others much easier. These could be a great starting point for deciding what your business will be. Dame Anita Roddick started up her business, The Body Shop®, after realizing a passion for producing and retailing beauty products that prohibited the use of ingredients tested on animals. Maurice and Charles Saatchi founded the advertising agency Saatchi and Saatchi after gaining years of experience and skills, along with influential contacts in the world of advertising.

Contents

About the authors

Alex Ritchie runs Alex Ritchie Consulting and is also co-founder and director of Venn Street, which has been project managing and delivering the Global Entrepreneurship Week campaign on behalf of the UK hosts. She is an advisory board member for Astia, a global organization that propels women's participation as entrepreneurs and business leaders, and a UK advisory board member of Finca, a global microfinance institute providing financial services to the world's lowest-income entrepreneurs. In addition to being a trained coach, she previously worked in the business support sector advising businesses, and is passionate about connecting people and inspiring them to reach their potential.

Natalie Campbell is founder and director of A Very Good Company, an innovation agency that works with businesses such as Virgin Media, Channel 4 and Marks and Spencer to drive social change in communities around the world. Natalie is also a Trustee of UnLtd, the Foundation for Social Entrepreneurs, and a board member of Wayra UnLtd, a technology accelerator programme created by Telefonia. Having started her first business at nineteen, by twenty-one she was juggling studying for a degree and starting up a Morgan De Toi retail franchise. Natalie has used her experience to champion global entrepreneurship development, taking the stage in Vietnam and Jamaica. She is also a business commentator for the BBC and sector press.

Step 1

KNOW YOUR BUSINE

'The secret of getting ahead is getting started.' — Mark Twain (1835–1910), American author

Five ways to succeed

■ Start a business you believe in.

■ Use your skills, experience and contacts.

■ Be ambitious with your vision and aims.

■ Identify what differentiates your business – your USP.

■ Understand your market and customers.

Five ways to fail

■ Underestimate your customer.

■ Believe you'll get rich quickly.

■ Assume you can work all day, every day.

■ Fail to make the most of your network.

■ Ignore the tax man.

Contents

About the authors

Alex Ritchie runs Alex Ritchie Consulting and is also co-founder and director of Venn Street, which has been project managing and delivering the Global Entrepreneurship Week campaign on behalf of the UK hosts. She is an advisory board member for Astia, a global organization that propels women's participation as entrepreneurs and business leaders, and a UK advisory board member of Finca, a global microfinance institute providing financial services to the world's lowest-income entrepreneurs. In addition to being a trained coach, she previously worked in the business support sector advising businesses, and is passionate about connecting people and inspiring them to reach their potential.

Natalie Campbell is founder and director of A Very Good Company, an innovation agency that works with businesses such as Virgin Media, Channel 4 and Marks and Spencer to drive social change in communities around the world. Natalie is also a Trustee of UnLtd, the Foundation for Social Entrepreneurs, and a board member of Wayra UnLtd, a technology accelerator programme created by Telefonia. Having started her first business at nineteen, by twenty-one she was juggling studying for a degree and starting up a Morgan De Toi retail franchise. Natalie has used her experience to champion global entrepreneurship development, taking the stage in Vietnam and Jamaica. She is also a business commentator for the BBC and sector press.

Step 1
KNOW YOUR BUSINESS

'The secret of getting ahead is getting started.' — Mark Twain (1835–1910), American author

Five ways to succeed

Start a business you believe in.

Use your skills, experience and contacts.

Be ambitious with your vision and aims.

Identify what differentiates your business – your USP.

Understand your market and customers.

Five ways to fail

Underestimate your customer.

Believe you'll get rich quickly.

Assume you can work all day, every day.

Fail to make the most of your network.

Ignore the tax man.

What kind of business will you run?

So, you know that you want to run your own business. You have a few ideas in mind that get you excited but how do you decide where to start?

Your passion, skills and experience

Take a good look at yourself. Is there something you're particularly passionate about? Have you always wondered whether you could turn your passion into a business? You may have a talent or skill which would enable you to start a business in a certain field, such as hairdressing or baking. Or you might be a professional, such as a lawyer, dentist or physiotherapist, and have realized that, rather than working for someone else, you now have the skills and experience to set up your own practice. Alternatively, you have identified a problem in your community that you think you might just have a solution for, or maybe you've come up with an idea that would make your life or the lives of others much easier. These could be a great starting point for deciding what your business will be. Dame Anita Roddick started up her business, The Body Shop®, after realizing a passion for producing and retailing beauty products that prohibited the use of ingredients tested on animals. Maurice and Charles Saatchi founded the advertising agency Saatchi and Saatchi after gaining years of experience and skills, along with influential contacts in the world of advertising.

You've chosen the idea – what's next?

Vision

You should create a vision for your business. Your vision is what you describe to people when explaining your idea, and it should be easily understood by those you want to sell to. It can be big and aspirational or it can be succinct and to the point. It should be your inspiration for the future of the company. It's worth reading about the vision your competitors have or the vision behind brands that you really like; this will give you an understanding of what might work for your business. For example, when Bill Gates first started Microsoft, he envisioned a personal computer in every home and business.

Aims

The aims of your business are more practical and operational than your vision. They'll change over time as your business grows. Your aims will usually be two or three things that you hope your business will do. An aim might be something like 'sell 3,000 cupcakes in the first year' or 'supply my goods to a leading manufacturer in my industry by a specific date'. Having aims keeps you focused on what success looks like in a more manageable way than a vision, which might take years to fulfil.

Choosing a name

You've managed the hard part. You've come up with an idea that fulfils your passion and is potentially profitable. You've got a vision and aims. Now you need to think about a name. This helps to make your idea real so you can start sharing it and getting feedback on your concept. There's no science to this. You need a piece of paper, a pen and maybe a few friends, but start writing whatever comes to mind. Here are some things to consider.

■ Do you want a business name that says what it does on the tin?

■ Do you want to stand out with something less conventional or even radical?

■ Do you want to fit in with your competitors or is there an industry norm?

When considering the above, think about your industry sector, competitors and customers. This should help you to weigh the advantages and disadvantages of each. Once you've got a few names you like, ask people what they think; you can change your mind right up until the minute you register the business.

Different business types

Product- versus service-based business

Product-based businesses sell 'things' to their customers. They may sell to ordinary people like you and me: this is called business to consumer (B2C). On the other hand, they could sell to other businesses: this is called business to business (B2B). Popular B2C product-based businesses are retailers selling clothing, homeware, books, music, etc. In fact, the list is endless. B2B product-based businesses typically supply products that other businesses or institutions need as part of their own production process, for example, widgets, machinery, medical equipment, wholesale clothing and IT equipment.

Service-based businesses utilize your skills, time and talent. Think cleaning companies, day-care and consultancies. Service-based businesses can also be B2C or B2B.

Some businesses can sell both services and products, for example, cafés and restaurants. We see more and more of these service-based businesses acting as retailers, selling goods alongside core service. We discuss this further on page 12.

Both types of business might require start-up capital but if you're a product-based business, it's likely that you'll need to purchase goods and pay for distribution or premises, whereas many service-based businesses can be started on a shoestring.

Business to business or business to consumer

When it comes to choosing between business to business (B2B) and business to consumer (B2C), you might not have to. Both markets might be profitable and keep you busy throughout the year. Consider offering your services direct to customers *and* businesses. Take, for example, a café that supplies offices or offers large-scale catering services and caters for walk-in trade as well.

If you can service both markets, you're providing yourself with a much broader target market, which could help the business to succeed in difficult times. For example, if you were setting up a florist but found that a competitor or a local branch of a supermarket had set up over the road and was beginning to undercut your prices, you might be thankful that you'd started supplying to weddings and venues and built a relationship with the local funeral directors.

Setting up an online business

These days, starting a business online can be a low risk entry point. You don't even have to build your own website any more as third-party sites such as eBay™ and Etsy have created direct-to-market opportunities for people with products ready to ship. Starting online could be a good option if you're selling popular consumer items such as fashion or homeware. It's especially good if you need to test out how your market works and what people are willing to pay for, all without expensive overheads. There are a number of online business success stories, from Net-a-Porter to Notonthehighstreet.com and the global giant Amazon.

Location, location, location

Thinking about your location and business base isn't something that should be left to the last minute as it can make all the difference to your business thriving or even getting off the ground. If your clients or the industry you're working in are based in a different town or city to you, it's worth considering having an address or virtual office in the same area as this helps with credibility.

Here are a few things you should also consider.

■ **Global versus local**

   Will your business sell its products or services internationally or more locally in your neighbourhood or community? You might do both, which will take more effort and money, so think carefully before you decide upon world domination.

■ **Footfall on the high street**

   If you're setting up a physical shop, where's the best location for what you do? Do you need passing trade or do you work by appointment? If empty premises catch your eye, spend a few days counting how many people pass by at different times during the day as this will be your footfall if you had that space.

■ **Costs**

   If you have premises, you'll incur a number of costs, such as business rates, and you'll need public liability insurance (see page 93). Factor all of this in when planning as it adds up. Some areas have business incentive schemes; speak to the local Chamber of Commerce wherever you end up.

Networks and support

You know the old adage: 'It's not what you know, it's who you know'? Well, here's an updated version: 'It's not what you know, how much money you have or how brilliant you think your idea is, it's who you know that will be the difference between success and a hard old slog'. While that's a bit of a mouthful, in business it's true, and you'll find over time that networks and making connections might be even more important to your business than money.

Although in the UK the Government-backed business support environment has shrunk somewhat over the last few years during the economic recession, there are still organizations out there that can help you to get your business idea off the ground. In the UK, look at organizations such as the National Enterprise Network, UK Trade and Investment, and Chambers of Commerce. Most of these will have local branches and some offer access to finance alongside advice.

Networks and networking

As you start working on your business, the opportunities for growing your network will increase and you'll make connections all the time, for example, with suppliers, customers or other local businesses. It's important to seize these opportunities and find out if there are any networking events that might be available for you to attend in your industry sector or your local area.

Networking tips

- **Play nice**

  It's important to play nice when networking as bullish over-sellers who take without giving are often shunned or seen as people not worth doing business with.

- **Give more**

  Give more than you get in order to create a strong group of business connections that will take your call night or day and help you to win contracts, sell products or just listen and share advice when times are tough.

- **Stay connected**

  It's nice to check in with people from time to time without asking anything of them. Drop them an email or give them a call for a chat or to arrange a coffee. Alternatively, there are some great social media tools that help you to stay connected with the people you meet out and about. LinkedIn® is a great way of sharing and staying in contact with your network, as is Facebook, depending on the sort of business you run. Find out what works for your industry and get online.

Money, money, money

Ah! We find ourselves on the all-too-important topic of money. It's a fact that without it your business won't get very far, but how do you get enough to get started, and what should you spend it on? As part of your business planning process, make a list of necessary purchases and expenditure required in order to start up and run your business. (See Step 6.)

Money to get the business up and running

There are four main ways most people get enough money to get their idea off the ground and catapulted into a fully-fledged business. Of course, it all depends on the scale of your operation and whether or not you need to buy stock, set up an office or work internationally. But it's a good start to know the main sources.

Savings and personal finance

The vast majority of people start their business using personal savings of some sort. If you intend to start small or run your business alongside having a job, this might be a good option for you as there is less risk involved and you're accountable only to yourself for recouping the money.

Family and friends

Family and friends are the next most common source of business funding. They're a good source of finance to start with if you need a few thousand pounds to set up premises or buy stock. It's always worth considering the worst case scenario, however: what happens if you can't pay back the money? What would happen if they wanted their money back early? Do you want them getting involved in the day-to-day affairs of your business? The best course of action is to set up an investor agreement – a legally binding document outlining the amount of investment, the payment terms and any involvement the investor may have in the management of the company. As a minimum, have some form of written contract outlining what would happen in each case and what you are liable for. You don't want your twenty-year friendship to break down as a result of borrowing money without clear expectations to begin with.

Banks

If you need a large cash outlay to begin with, it's worth setting up a meeting with a business banking manager to find out what they can offer you in terms of loans or overdraft facilities. They'll want to see a business plan (see Step 2) and might even give you a template to use.

If you need larger amounts of capital to purchase stock or you need to buy what banks call assets, for example, machinery, cars and property, you may need a loan to get moving. It's worth noting that banks in the UK, for example, don't seem to be lending money on the same scale as they were a few years ago, so go fully prepared and be ready for detailed questions and knock-backs.

Lending circles and crowd funding

Lending circles and crowd funding are a relatively new phenomenon. The principle here is that lots of people give small amounts of money that count towards your total loan. It works well for creative businesses or social enterprises that can target people who are interested in the cause behind what the business or enterprise does. Depending on the platform, the money might be an investment or given in return for a first run of products. Benefits could include lower interest rates and the ability to obtain funding which cannot be raised through more traditional methods. As lending circles and crowd funding are relatively new, you should fully research these funding methods in your country and read the terms and conditions of the organization you intend to approach to ensure you are aware of any fees or claims on the intellectual property of your business.

Business angels and venture capitalists

Business angels (angels) and venture capitalists (VCs) are third parties that will invest in your business for a return on the profits. They're looking for businesses with high growth potential that will provide them with a good return on their investment (ROI) and in general, will invest substantial amounts of money. There are a number of hoops you'll have to jump through, which will vary depending on the investor. You'll need a watertight business plan for the first three to five years of business, details of your supply chain, customers and finances (see Step 2), and you'll need to prepare proposals and pitches (see Step 4).

Angels tend to invest smaller amounts, typically from tens of thousands up to around £250,000. They'll take an interest in you and your team as well as your idea but will have an exit strategy and time frame in mind. They often bring contacts and networks and may request a non-executive director position.

VCs typically look to invest millions for a share of the company. Invariably, they will only invest in businesses that show potential to grow very quickly, with strong management teams and proven business models. This option will probably not be right for you at this stage but there's no harm in thinking big.

It's best to go through established angel and VC networks or agencies. There are a number of these agencies available for different sectors or locations, so use the internet to research them. Their fees or commission on the investment will vary. It's worth checking out www.angelsden.com.

Registering your business

You have a vision, you've identified your aims, market and USP, you've thought of a name and secured funding, and now you're ready to register your business. In the UK, this is done at Companies House. The legal term for this is incorporating your business. It's a fairly simple procedure which can be done online, and all of the information you need can be found at www.companieshouse.gov.uk. If you've already appointed an accountant, it may be worth asking them to incorporate your business for you as this is usually a service that's offered by accountants for a small fee.

Registering the business name

Although you may have chosen a name you like, you must also check that it's not already being used by a registered company. There are websites and organizations that will offer to check your chosen name for you for a fee, and in the UK you can do your own search for free using the Companies House web checker facility. It's worth remembering that registering a company name does not automatically give you trademark protection on that name. Further information on registering a trademark can be found in Step 2.

Company structures in the UK

When setting up a business in the UK, you need to decide on the legal structure, which will depend on how you will be running the company. Talk to other business owners to understand why they opted for a certain structure and ask them about the pros and cons. The table below outlines the most common types of companies registered.

Company type	What does this mean?
Sole trader	The business is owned entirely by you, although you may decide to employ other people. As a sole trader you have unlimited liability, which means that you are personally liable for any debts or losses. One benefit of this structure is that there is less paperwork and fewer formality requirements involved in setting up. This type of business often works well for freelancers or independent consultants.
Limited company (Ltd)	The most common version of a limited company is a private company limited by shares. The business is a separate legal entity to its directors. All profits are owned by the company. Company directors aren't personally responsible for debts the business can't pay if it goes wrong. Limited companies benefit from a lower tax rate than sole traders. Many businesses fall into this category, from builders to restaurants, and shops to marketing agencies.
Limited Liability Partnership (LLP)	LLPs are most commonly set up by professional services firms, for example, solicitors or accountants. In a LLP, the partners do not bear legal or financial responsibility for the business, unlike ordinary partnerships or limited partnerships, where partners may be responsible for debts or losses.

Tax

Corporation tax

So, you now have an incorporated company, which means you must also register for corporation tax. This can be done as a joint procedure with the business incorporation process if you chose the Companies House web incorporation process. Either way, in the UK, you must by law tell Her Majesty's Revenue and Customs (HMRC) that your company or organization is 'active' within three months of starting business activity. HMRC offer an online registration process at www.hmrc.gov.uk, where they also explain how and when to complete tax returns.

Value added tax

As well as corporation tax, you may need to register for value added tax (VAT). In the UK, legally you don't need to register for VAT until your business has made taxable sales of over £79,000 in the previous twelve months (this is true at the time of writing) but there might be benefits to registering for VAT voluntarily even if your sales are lower than this amount. For example, if you purchase a reasonably large amount of goods or services for the business, you will be able to claim back the VAT on these purchases.

It's worth considering your options and discussing the pros and cons with an accountant. In addition, the VAT thresholds change yearly and have some exceptions, such as (but not exclusively) businesses which are distance selling, either online or by mail order.

Setting up a business bank account

It's worth setting up a bank account as soon as you register your business as it can take a lot longer to set up than a personal bank account and may well involve a face-to-face meeting with a business, bank manager.

In the UK, banks usually make monthly charges to businesses in order to operate their account and charge for specific services. Which bank you decide to use is your choice but when researching the marketplace, these are the main things to consider.

■ Do they offer a period of discounted or free banking for start-ups?

■ Do you need an account that allows you to accept or send payments in different currencies?

■ Is it important that your business uses a bank with an 'ethical' reputation or one which works in 'charitable' ways?

■ Do you need local branches to pay in cash or cheques?

■ Will your business require an overdraft facility?

Most banks now offer online and telephone banking, which are a must for most businesses these days. If you have decided not to use one of the big high street banks, do check what the smaller banks offer in terms of online and telephone banking.

Key take-aways

Think about the things you will take away from Step 1 and how you will implement them.

Topic	Take-away	Implementation
Deciding what kind of business to run	• *Understanding my passions, skills and experience will help me to decide what my business will do.* • *Think about the practicalities of running a business.*	• *Draw up a list of my skills, experience and passions.* • *Make a list of the pros and cons for my business idea.*
Identifying your USP		
Creating a vision and aims for your business		
Choosing a suitable name for your business		
Deciding on a location for your business		
Using networking to help your business		
Financing the start-up of your business		
Registering your business		
Registering for tax		
Setting up a business bank account		

Step 2

FORM A BUSINESS PLAN

'Failing to plan is planning to fail.'
— Alan Lakein, author

Five ways to succeed

Use all available resources to help you to research.

Put your best foot forward.

Be completely honest when doing your SWOT.

Understand what your customers really need.

Seek expert advice when you need it.

Five ways to fail

Waffle and use jargon.

Assume you know your market and competitors.

Cut corners when doing research and analysis.

Fail to get the maths right.

Write your business plan and then ignore it.

What is a business plan?

Put simply, a business plan is a set of goals and a roadmap of how you will achieve them. You may be wondering why you need a business plan, especially if you're starting up a very small business, perhaps with only yourself working for it, and aren't planning on borrowing any money to finance it. Well, the answer is simple: writing down your goals and plans will allow you to focus more clearly on your idea and spot any gaps or opportunities that you may not previously have been aware of. In addition, it provides you with a written set of time-specific goals for the business to be working towards, allowing you to track its progress. And of course, if you're seeking investment or a loan, your bank or other potential investors will want to see a business plan and they will be your key readership.

You don't have to be a financial expert or an experienced strategist to write an effective business plan. Indeed, your first one could be very simple and only a few pages in length.

How to do your research

It's likely that you'll need to do some research to complete your business plan. Research is often a confusing area for new entrepreneurs, so don't be afraid to ask for help.

A good place to start is at the library: try the business section, which should contain useful resources, such as industry sector reference books or databases with information on the size of the market, detailed information on your competitors and market trends. Some cities have business and patent libraries that hold a vast stock of up-to-date reference books and databases on all industry sectors. In the UK, the biggest one is the British Library in London. Other cities throughout the UK and internationally have similar resources; check out the European PatLib network. Alternatively, try the Institute of Directors, which has an international network of branches and affiliates, or relevant trade associations, for example, the Chartered Institute of Marketing. These organizations can help you to get your idea off the ground by providing information on trademarking, intellectual property and in-depth information on your industry sector.

The internet is also a goldmine of intelligence, and there are hundreds of websites providing tools or templates to help you to do your research or write your business plan.

The all-important executive summary

Let's begin with the summary of your business plan. Although you're likely to write this section after you've completed the rest of the plan, it should appear at the beginning of your plan, so we'll cover it here.

This is the single most important part of your plan and where you can capture your readers' attention. Keep it clear, succinct and engaging. Anyone reviewing your plan will read this section first before deciding if they're interested enough to keep reading.

In this section you should introduce yourself and describe your experience and any relevant skills or qualifications. Give a brief description of the business, its purpose and a summary headline overview of how this will be achieved. Highlight the following aspects of the business:

- its strengths, for example, its USP, any intellectual property or registered trademarks held, upfront orders, management team experience
- expected profitability and turnover
- the market and the potential for sales
- any funding requirements and potential prospects for investors

The length of your summary will depend on the length and complexity of your business plan. As a general rule of thumb, an acceptable length is somewhere between one and four pages. Before writing yours, it's worth reading a few others to compare length, style and detail. Larger businesses often include their business plan on the company website, so look around at how others have written their executive summaries. If you're writing your business plan to leverage investment, ask your potential investors if they have a particular style or format you should adhere to.

Business description

The business description section usually follows on from the executive summary. It should outline the vital elements of the business, including:

- a history of the business or the history of the idea.

- the ownership of the business.

- any awards won or membership in reputable industry bodies.

- the location of the business.

- the structure of the business (e.g. sole trader, Ltd, LLP).

- the company size.

- the purpose of the business or mission statement if one has been developed.

- your vision.

Be careful not to use industry or business jargon when describing these things as the reader may not understand it. Keep descriptions simple, using layman's language.

Description of the products or services

Next, you need to describe your product or service. What does it offer the customer and why should they buy it? Does it have any unusual or innovative features? How will you make the product or run the service? How will orders be fulfilled? Make a brief comparison to any similar products or services on the market and describe what makes yours unique. If you have any intangible assets, such as trademarks, copyright or patents pending or owned, ensure you describe them here.

Market analysis

Your target market

Next, you need to think about the demographics of your customers. Think about their age range(s), location, gender, social groups, lifestyle preferences, purchasing habits, income level, education, hobbies, and indeed anything you can find that will help to define their characteristics as closely as possible. You must analyse each sub-group of your target market and develop a different marketing plan to reach each of them. (See Step 3.)

Include the size of your target market and what the purchase potential might be (gathered from your market research and analysis – see page 31). Have you identified any key purchasing motivations that a particular group has? Do they need your product or service or is there a problem that it will alleviate? If so, include it. Where statistics or graphs are available, include them and reference where they came from. Trade associations and industry bodies can be useful here; they represent particular industries and trades, and it's likely that there'll be one for your industry or trade too.

Lastly, you need to provide information on how you expect to reach the market – your marketing strategy. Information later on in this step and in Step 3 will help you to define this.

Market research

It's important that you carry out market research on your business idea, products or services so that you get a good idea of how well they'll be received by your potential customers.

There are two basic kinds of market research, quantitative and qualitative, and there are a number of different methods within each of the two categories. Both types can provide useful information and you might decide on a mixture of both, depending on your budget or time frame. Generally, qualitative research provides more detailed results from fewer people and can take more time, money or resources per person to conduct, whereas quantitative research usually provides less detailed information from much larger numbers of people within a shorter time frame and often at a cheaper rate. You should aim to use a mixture of both types to ensure you achieve reliable results from your research.

Qualitative

■ **Focus groups**

Gather a group of potential customers together to garner their opinions on any aspect of your business. Questions should be structured according to what information you wish to learn. For example, if you need to understand what will make your customers buy your product, ask them what they currently buy that's similar and why they buy it. Include questions about convenience, price, brand allegiance, customer service, etc. Then ask them what they like and don't like about your particular product.

■ **In-depth interviews**

One-to-one interviews can provide more detailed results but will require a longer time frame or a larger team of interviewers.

■ **Field trials**

These involve placing your product with a group of customers or stores and allowing them to test it for a specified period of time. This can be very effective but ensure you obtain agreement beforehand that customers or stores will be willing to feed back results in a structured way. This could involve contacting a group of potential or existing customers and asking them if they'd like to trial your product for free for a period of time in return for completing a short survey on their findings.

Quantitative

■ **Surveys**

Surveys can reach a larger number of people. Distribution might be in hard copy or online or conducted via telephone or in person. You should be prepared for fairly low response rates (5% would be considered a good response rate if you're not offering an incentive for completing the survey) and less detailed responses.

Data collection and analysis

Data collection and analysis is also known as a situational analysis and is a vital part of business planning, involving the collection and evaluation of data about your own business, those of your competitors and the wider sector. Completing this particular element of the business plan will:

■ provide you with the evidence you need on which to base your forecasts.

■ help you to decide which opportunities to pursue, along with the strengths and weaknesses of your business or products.

■ enable you to identify any competitive advantage you have.

The situational analysis enables you to evaluate the position of your business, idea or products. There are various tools that can be used but the following are the four key tools.

PEST analysis

PEST is an acronym for political, economic, social and technological factors. A PEST analysis generally looks at external factors and can help you to understand changes or developments in the market and the position of your business in it by looking at the 'bigger picture'. It'll help you to identify external opportunities or threats and take proactive action. We look at each factor in turn here.

Political factors

Political factors relate to Government and include anything related to the law or legislation, for example, employment law and health and safety. Each country has its own set of legislation. Information on UK legislative acts can be found at: www.legislation.gov.uk. How might these affect your business?

Economic factors

Economic factors relate to things like interest rates or changes in inflation. How might the way the economy is performing affect your business?

Social factors

Social factors relate to consumer spending habits and trends. These are, of course, linked to economic factors as you're likely to find that people's spending habits go down in a recession and up in a boom. How might they affect your business?

Technical factors

Technical factors relate to advances in technology that could enable your business to run more efficiently, reach a wider number of customers or fulfil orders faster.

Here is an example of a PEST analysis.

PEST analysis for a new delicatessen business			
Political	**Economic**	**Social**	**Technical**
• Food hygiene regulations • Employment law • Tax situation unknown	• Local economy growth up by 4% over the last 2 years • Local area has higher than average earnings	• Eating out is a form of recreation • There's a strong local business network	• Good local broadband provision • Smartphone use high – use social media to generate awareness

Once you have a completed grid, consider what each element under the four sections might mean to your business. For example, if the tax situation is unknown, it's important to clarify this quickly. If there is good local broadband provision, maybe you could you offer free Wi-Fi to your customers.

SWOT analysis

SWOT is an acronym for strengths, weaknesses, opportunities and threats. Generally, strengths and weaknesses are internal factors, and opportunities and threats are external factors. Be clear about what you're analysing, for example, the business idea, a new product or a new service. Then begin to list all the findings under each section. This exercise is often more effective when performed as part of a team exercise or brainstorm.

Completing a SWOT analysis is simple: create a 2 x 2 grid with each of the four headings in one of the boxes.

SWOT analysis for a new delicatessen business	
Strengths 1 Strong ethical values 2 High quality, locally sourced produce 3 Homemade cakes, breads and pies	**Weaknesses** 1 25% more expensive than other local cafés 2 Brand unknown in the marketplace
Opportunities 1 No local businesses offering high quality and range of goods 2 Local producers keen to supply	**Threats** 1 Increase in global food prices could put delicatessen prices out of customers' reach 2 Market demand can be seasonal

Once you have completed the grid, consider how you'll leverage the strengths and opportunities, mitigate the risk of threats and make changes to reduce your weaknesses. For example:

Strengths, point 1: Emphasize your ethical values in all marketing and promotional materials and describe why they are a positive element of the business.

Weaknesses, point 1: Why is this? Are you using higher quality ingredients? Is the delicatessen a luxury or aspirational place? If so, ensure that your customers understand this. Maybe you're paying high prices for ingredients and need to look at alternative suppliers.

Competitive analysis

Wouldn't it be nice if you were the only business supplying your products or services to your ideal customers? Of course it would, but unless you've managed to come up with a brand-new innovation, it's highly unlikely that you'll have that luxury. Therefore, you need to understand as much as possible about your competitors so that you can differentiate your business and offering.

Make a list of all the products and services you plan to provide, along with your customer base for each. Now add a list of other organizations supplying similar products and services to the same customer base. You may already know many of your competitors but don't take it for granted that you know them all. Use the places and resources mentioned in **How to do your research** on page 27 to ensure that you haven't missed any new competitors or others who may be expanding their offering and stepping into your market.

Now begin looking at their offerings: what are their strengths and weaknesses? Are they more or less expensive than you and do they offer additional services that you don't? Where does your business sit in relation to its competitors and where do you want to be? Why are your competitors ahead of you? How do they reach their customers?

It's also worth understanding the perceived value of your competitors' brand and the quality of their offering. If you happen to be in an industry where customer reviews are available online, check them out to see what people like or dislike about your competitors.

Marketing strategy

Detailed marketing is covered in Step 3, but you need to outline how you intend to approach this within the business plan.

The 4 Ps of marketing

E. J. McCarthy was an American marketing professor who proposed the concept of the four Ps – product, price, place and promotion – and the way they guide the marketing mix. This is a business tool used in marketing, and will enable you to break down the marketing variables into the four Ps mentioned above and help you to achieve results in your specific target market. You should provide detailed information under each 'P' heading, which will be different for every business in every industry.

Product

What is the product name and what does it look like? (size, colour, texture, etc.)

What can you say about its functionality, including special features? What needs does it satisfy?

How and where will the customer use it?

How is it different from anything else on the market?

What is the maximum cost of production in order for it to still make a profit?

Does it have any warranties and quality marks?

What information is there on the packaging? (materials, size, cost, etc.)

Price

Is there flexibility within your pricing or are there industry-established price points for products or services? Look at what your competitors are charging.

How have you worked out your prices? Look at the type of strategies most commonly used in your sector and consider discounts for retail, trade, bulk purchases, etc.

Is there a maximum price your customers would be willing or able to pay? (You will cover this in your market research.)

Place

What are your distribution channels? Are there others you need to consider?

Where will you sell the product or service? Will this be online, at trade fairs, in shops or through a sales team?

Have you organized all necessary logistics and transportation (if transporting physical products)?

Do your competitors do anything differently? If so, it might be worth looking into this further.

What are your order processing and fulfilment systems?

Promotion

What are the best ways to reach your customers? (advertising, direct marketing, the internet, public relations, etc.)

Have you defined your marketing budget? This could minimize the use of some of the more expensive methods of marketing.

What promotional activities do your competitors use?

Management and organization

In many cases, this part of the business plan will be quite short for a start-up business. It's unlikely that you'll have a sizeable management team at this stage or even a fully formed staff team. However, it's still worth including this section and highlighting the company structure and your own involvement, skills and attributes. If you've already employed staff or have defined some of the roles that will need filling, draw up a simple organizational chart (also known as an organogram) to show this. Here is an example of what this might look like.

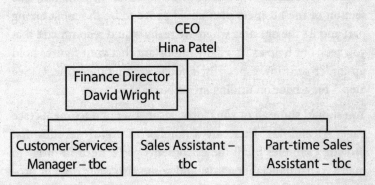

You should also include information on how the business will be run. For example, do your senior managers have autonomy to run their departments as they see fit or does the CEO make all of the decisions? What sort of targets do the teams or employees have? What's your planned recruitment process? For example, will you use a recruitment agency, advertise in local, trade or national press, use the job centre, or will you use temporary staff until the orders are more consistent?

Financial analysis

Your new business won't have any financial history, so the information you provide within this section will be your estimates based upon what you know of the market and your customers. All of the research and analysis you've completed up to this point will really help you to forecast for the future. It may seem a little strange to be making assumptions on financial forecasts but it's quite acceptable to do so as long as you're consistent and can provide evidence.

If you aren't used to working with financial information, this section of the business plan could prove to be the most taxing part and it's the one area where we really would recommend that you seek out help as it's vitally important that your figures hold up under scrutiny, especially if you're seeking investment. (See Step 5 for advice on finding an accountant.)

You should show all of your forecasts in a set of documents (see pages 41 and 42). There are a number of useful websites that provide examples of all the documents you'll need in order to make your financial analysis, and some also offer help in projecting your figures. These include: www.startupdonut.co.uk, www.projectionhub.com and www.accountingcoach.com.

Sales forecast

To estimate how many sales you'll make over the period, use the information from your market analysis, particularly the size and economic activity of the market, along with any relevant buying or growth trends. Consider how you see sales growing as you become more established and take on a larger share of the marketplace, for example, how many more customers do you expect to reach through your marketing and promotional activities? Any information that you have gleaned in your market research on market demand or customer buying behaviours will also be very useful here. For example:

	Year 1	Year 2
Unit sales		
Beverages	80,000	120,000
Hot food	20,000	35,000
Cold food	40,000	55,000
Total unit sales	140,000	210,000
Unit prices		
Beverages	£1.50	£1.55
Hot food	£5	£5.20
Cold food	£3	£3.10
Sales (value)		
Beverages	£120,000	£186,000
Hot food	£100,000	£182,000
Cold food	£120,000	£170,500
Total sales	£340,000	£538,500

Profit and loss account

Your profit and loss (P&L) account will forecast turnover (in other words, your income) against the cost of any sales. This in turn will show the expected gross profit (before tax has been deducted) and net profit (after tax has been deducted) that you hope to make.

In order to complete the P&L account, you'll need to collate the following information for the given period:

- all income earned

- all costs, split into cost of sales plus all other costs, for example, accountancy fees, insurance, bank charges, rent, stationery, travel

- any interest received from banks or investments

Balance sheet

A balance sheet shows what your business is worth at any given time, so in the case of the business plan it's worth also compiling a forecast balance sheet for the end of each year it covers. The balance sheet will show the value of your owned assets, such as cash, buildings, vehicles, stock and equipment, and the value of your liabilities, such as suppliers' costs, interest on debts and salaries.

In order to complete the balance sheet, you'll need to collate the following information for the given period:

- all money in the business bank accounts and petty cash

- the value of stock, buildings, vehicles and equipment

- the value of invoices the business has raised to clients but that haven't yet been paid

- money owed to suppliers

- any taxes due during the given period

- money to be paid to company directors

- bank or other loans, or borrowed money

- money invested by shareholders

Financing requirements

This section is only necessary if you're seeking external investment from a bank or other financial organization.

You must lay out clearly how much investment you're looking for and exactly how you intend to use it. Refer to your research and analysis and your financial analysis as much as possible to support your request, and provide evidence for why you need the investment. If you're raising additional money through personal or other means, ensure you explain this and detail the amounts and any payment terms.

Your potential investor is going to want assurances that they'll get their initial investment back along with any agreed interest payments, so be clear how and when you expect to pay them.

Key take-aways

Think about the things you will take away from Step 2 and how you will implement them.

Topic	Take-away	Implementation
How to research	• *Understand what resources are available to support me locally.* • *Think about what the gaps in my knowledge are.*	• *Contact local libraries, trade associations or business support organizations to see how and where they can help.* • *Plan my research in advance.*
Creating an executive summary		
Describing your business, products and services		
Describing who your customers are and what they need		
Planning market research		
Analysing your business's position and its competitors		
Planning a marketing strategy		
Providing financial analysis		

Step 3

CREATE YOUR IDENTITY

'You can create a business, choose a name, but unless people know about it, you're not going to sell any products.' — Richard Branson, businessman and entrepreneur

Five ways to succeed

Create a business and brand with personality.

Use professional designers for a well-thought-out logo.

Get the right marketing materials before you launch.

Engage with your customers face to face.

Maintain your website.

Five ways to fail

Design a logo without considering your brand.

Copy the brand of your closest competitor.

Ignore feedback about your brand and logo design.

Spend money on marketing materials you don't need.

Don't bother to update your online presence regularly.

Brand basics

The most successful businesses, both big and small, have one thing in common: they have a strong brand that keeps customers coming back for more. A brand is more than a logo; it's the personality of your business.

Think about your business as a human being for one moment. What does it sound like? What does it look like? What does it believe in? How does it dress? How does it make your customers feel? That's what a brand evokes in people's minds, whether they consciously know it or not. Your customers aren't just interacting with your product or service; they are interacting with your brand and its personality. You need to keep this in mind as you bring your brand to life in a visual form, usually through an 'identity' or logo and its supporting 'brand assets'.

Businesses invest millions of pounds creating the right brand visuals and subliminal messages that tell everyone how great they are. You don't need tons of cash to do the same; you just need to spend a bit of time getting it right in the beginning.

Building a brand

A logo is not a brand

The most common mistake people make at this stage is asking someone to design a logo of the company name, or even worse, mocking something up themselves in five minutes on a computer. This is because lots of people think that designing a logo is the same as creating a brand.

Building a brand takes time and thought and shouldn't be undertaken lightly. If you're a visual person and you feel that having a logo and business cards will give you more confidence in your idea, schedule an afternoon to work on brand identity and what you want your business to stand for. Then share your ideas with friends to get that all-important feedback.

Think about a business that you bought something from in the last month. You'll probably visualise the product you bought, and then the logo or the slogan might pop into your head. What words spring to mind when you think about the business and its brand? Go one step further: think about the colours, sounds, music, people (maybe celebrities or the founder) and feelings you associate with the business. Now let's take a well-known brand like Apple. Inc. You'll probably think about Steve Jobs and all of the 'i' products: the apple logo, the clean design, etc. This is all the result of careful design. Scores of people in brand and design agencies work to give a logo a personality and meaning so that it becomes a brand. A brand has more selling power than just a logo. So if you want your business to be successful, build a brand. Don't just design a logo.

Identifying the personality of your business

The most recognizable brands in the world have spent a lot of time and money creating the right impression and giving you a brand experience. Fortunately, there are a few tricks of the trade that mean you don't have to spend millions to achieve the same effect. You'll need to have a vision and aims, and of course you'll have to have decided on a name first as that's the foundation of any good brand.

Before designing a logo or creating a strapline for your business, there are some things you should do. Your first task is to come up with a definition or values for your brand. This will help you to develop your 'brand association', in other words, the images and symbols associated with a brand or the benefits of a brand. Write down all of the words you'd like people to think of when they think about your business. You might include words like *reliable, beautiful* or *ethical* on your list. Now think about how you want people to feel when they come into contact with your business. For example, if you were setting up an adventure travel agency, you might write the words *energized, excited* or *adrenaline*. If you're not having much luck with this task or you're not good at getting creative, ask a friend to help you.

Now you've got your list, you need to create a visual board or mood board that brings the words to life. Think of your business as a person: where would it eat, shop, hang out? You can cut pictures out of magazines or create an online clipboard using Pinterest.com or Sharesquare.com. If you're working with a designer to create the logo and other visuals, this will help them to do a better job of designing something that really works for you.

Giving your business an identity

So, you've got a good understanding of how you want people to think and feel about your business. You've even got visuals that bring the words to life. Now you're ready to think about your business identity, more commonly referred to as the logo.

The logo

It's worth putting some budget aside to have your logo professionally designed. If you don't know any designers, ask people in your network if they can recommend anyone or search for experienced freelancers on LinkedIn® or Twitter. Beyond getting a great-looking visual, you'll also get 'brand assets'; these are things like colour palettes that suit your logo, different versions of your logo so you can use it online, in print and 3D if required. At this stage, you'll need to decide if you want to have an image (Apple Inc.) or your business name in words (Virgin Group Ltd.) or a mix of the two (PUMA®). Have a look at brands you like for inspiration and keep in mind what you want your overall brand to say to people.

If you decide to use a designer to get the best results, you should give them a brief that includes the brand associations you have created, the visual boards and your executive summary so they understand exactly what your business does and the industry you'll be operating in. They'll usually prepare three or four different ideas for you to choose from before spending time on one concept, which will ultimately be your final design.

The strapline

Another consideration is whether or not you want to have a strapline or slogan. This is usually a message attached to your logo that helps to define your brand. KFC has 'It's Finger Lickin' Good' and McDonald's uses 'I'm lovin' it'. The trends for straplines vary by industry; the food and retail industries use them a lot and they sometimes change as they refresh their brands. Technology-based businesses tend to go with quirky names over straplines.

Road-testing your brand

Before you print lots of materials, you should road-test your logo, strapline and brand assets with potential customers. If you don't have any assets, try and mock up some example web pages or promotional materials yourself. If that's not possible, ask family and friends to help out. You should ask them a few of the following questions.

- What do you think my business does based on what the logo looks like?

- Do you like it? If yes, why? If not, why not?

- What words come to mind when you look at the brand?

- Does the logo look like anything you've seen before?

- Do you think the logo works well online? (Ask only if you have web visuals to show, of course.)

Trademarks and copyright

Large companies usually trademark their logos to protect against other businesses stealing customers because the brands look and feel similar. You might not need to do this if you're setting up as a freelancer or one-man or one-woman band but if you're thinking about growing quickly, working internationally or selling products which can be copied by competitors, then it's worth exploring setting up a trademark or getting the copyright for any images or artwork associated with the brand or promotional materials.

Trademarks

A trademark is any sign that distinguishes your products and services from those of your competitors. You need to think about your brand as a whole and which bits you want to trademark. They can be specific words, logos or a combination of both. In the UK, you can apply for a trademark through the Intellectual Property Office. Each country will have its own registration body. There are a number of guidelines you'll need to follow, so it's worth seeking advice from the relevant body.

Copyright

Copyright protects written, theatrical, musical and artistic works as well as film, book layouts, sound recordings and broadcasts. Copyright is an automatic right, which means you don't have to apply for it but if you work with a designer, you need to make sure that *you* own the copyright to any materials they produce for you, not them. The terms of who owns the copyright should be in your contract with them, so check the contract thoroughly before the designer does any work for you.

Marketing your business online

Using the web to market yourself and your business is a cost-effective way of reaching new customers and keep existing ones coming back for more. The most important thing to remember is that whatever you say online is an extension of your brand, so go back to the list of words and images you created earlier and remember the personality you want to project. That's what needs to come alive online to market your business successfully.

You should also choose the most appropriate digital channels for your business, for example, a business website, blogs, apps, social networks and video platforms. Choosing the wrong channel means you could fall into the trap of building up a following that doesn't quite convert to sales but that you have to maintain some form of engagement with, which will take up time and possibly money. Think about your customers and ask yourself: do they use Facebook, Twitter or LinkedIn®? If so, you could use these to market your products and services. Or are they the kind of people who will buy directly from your website?

It's all too easy, for example, to track success as the number of Twitter followers or 'likes' you get each week, but if those followers and 'likes' aren't making you or your business any money, then essentially they're just taking up precious time that could be used on making actual sales. Yes, it's great to have an audience but it's even better to be able to pay the bills at the end of the month.

Getting started with a website

A good website is your first point of sale for people that might be searching for your products or services online. What they find there is a window into the sort of experience they'll have when they do business with you, so make sure you give your website the time and attention it deserves!

To register your website address, you'll need to use a domain registration agency like 123-Reg.com or 1and1.com. Both sites allow you to search listings to see what names are available for you to buy.

If you're setting up a consultancy, your website should include a list of the services you provide, client testimonials and links to articles you've written to highlight your expertise. If you're a retailer, it's likely that you'll need an e-commerce website so you can trade directly with customers through your site. To maximize sales, you should have pictures and written descriptions of your products, which will also help with search engine optimization (see page 54 for more information), and display costs clearly. The best way to ensure you have the right sort of website for your customers is to review what similar businesses have on their websites.

It's worth having a web designer help you to get a more bespoke look. If you don't know any web designers, ask around or search on LinkedIn® or Twitter. Or you can use a free template and add your own text and images. Have a look at moonfruit.com or weebly.com for a quick and simple way to create a professional-looking site.

Search engine optimization

A common term you'll see online when you're creating your site is search engine optimization (SEO). SEO is basically the process of making your website top of the list when people look for businesses like yours on search engines such as Google, Yahoo! and Bing. There are lots of ways to make this happen: using other social media and linking back to your website is a popular route to search engine stardom. Using keywords on your website or blog is another effective method (e.g. *cupcakes* if you run a bakery).

Make a list of all the words you'd associate with your business or that you think customers will use to look for you online. The more of them you can use when writing copy on your website, the better.

Using social media

A popular way of communicating with customers and giving them a fun way to engage with your brand is through the use of blogs, social networks and apps.

The great thing about using social media to market your brand is that you have both local and global reach from day one. But don't forget that social media is exactly that, social. There's a two-way conversation and customers can use it to give you an earful if they get bad service just as much as to lavish you with praise.

Here are some questions to think about before setting up social media channels.

What online channels do my customers use?

What sort of information do they share on these channels?

How often do they communicate?

What channel works best for my brand?

What channels do my competitors use? What sort of content (e.g. articles, pictures, video, reports) do they share?

Do I want to fit in with my competitors or create different content because it fits my brand better?

Do I have enough content or enough interesting things to share with my audience?

Do I have time to manage more than one channel?

This last point is key. Not only do you need to think about what is appropriate for your customers; you need to think about what you are able to achieve and not be overly ambitious.

Social networks for your business

Social networks are a great way to build your brand and make it come alive for your customers. As we've said, they can be a way to show off the personality of your business and can be a great tool to showcase products or build awareness of your expertise to a potentially global audience. The most popular social networks for business are Facebook, Twitter and LinkedIn®.

Facebook

You might already be up to speed with how to use Facebook, but using Facebook personally and using it to build and market your brand is another matter entirely. The main difference is that your business has a fan page with some very smart audience analytics thrown in for free. You can track what sort of content your 'friends' like and what sort of things they share. Facebook pages are great if you're selling products or running events as you can manage all of the content, post updates and invite people in one place.

Twitter

Twitter works well if you want to have instant conversations with your customers. A mobile coffee van used Twitter to set up a 'Tweet-your-order' service so customers didn't have to wait in the rain. They just tweeted their order and name and picked it up on the go. You might also use it to get feedback on products you're developing or to announce winning new clients.

Social networks for you

It's worth considering how you personally showcase your brand and the business you're trying to build. Increasingly, people search online for new contacts they've met in person in order to see how credible they are and to find out what their career history and experience is. One site that comes up most often all over the world is LinkedIn®.

LinkedIn®

LinkedIn® is a professional version of Facebook and most people list their career CV and links to their businesses or employers on their profile. You can add information about your business on a company page and it's a great tool to research competitors. You can also use it as a brand and personal marketing platform because your clients and customers can endorse your skills and the quality of service you provide and recommend you to other people.

To get the most out of LinkedIn®, you should remember the general tips about building a network in Step 1 and think about what valuable information you can upload onto your profile should anyone search for you online. Make sure your profile picture is professional; this isn't the place for that picture of you at a party with a blue wig on. A simple headshot would work well or a picture of you in action is even better. Why not give potential customers a real view of you at work?

Blogs

A blog is simply a written or visual update that you create to share information with customers, such as new product launches, top tips or industry insight. It's a great way to stay in contact with new and existing clients. If you decide to set one up, you'll need to schedule time to maintain it and you need to think carefully about what sort of things you'll share to keep people interested. Wordpress.com and Tumblr.com are great places to start and they have lots of guidance on how to get started. They both have templates and easy-to-use functions so you can update your blogs on the go.

Apps

Apps (short for 'applications') are like micro websites that usually run on a smartphone or tablet. There are two ways they might be beneficial at this stage: they'll either make marketing yourself easier or they'll help you to sell products. If you want to set up an appointments only boutique, wedding planning service or personal training business, for example, you might need an app that allows people to book in a session with you. If you're setting up a café or restaurant, you could use an app to help people to rate your food or service. This way, other people using the same app get to hear about you without you having to spend lots of money on advertising. Have a look through the business section of your app store, for example, the Apple App Store or Google Play, for a full list of what's available.

Using content platforms

Content-based platforms like YouTube allow you to show your customers exactly what they're paying for and why. The most popular platforms have the added benefit of millions of users and open your business up to potential customers almost overnight.

Pinterest

Pinterest is a free picture board that allows you to create a visual dashboard of all the products you sell or the things that inspire you to create. It's ideal if your business sells products directly to consumers.

YouTube

YouTube is a long-established video sharing platform that's great if you have videos from events or talks that you've done. You can also build a following by posting videos of yourself giving hints and tips about your area of expertise. If you're running a café or delicatessen, for example, you could video yourself creating some culinary delights.

Vimeo

Vimeo is similar to YouTube but it has a big community of film-makers and creatives, so it's perfect as a place to show your first short film or edits from an animation.

Marketing your business offline

It can't be stressed enough that *people buy from people*, so it's crucial that you balance your online marketing with more personal methods. As previously mentioned, building networks and networking is a great first step but you might also consider attending industry trade events to showcase your business and meet prospective buyers.

Word of mouth and recommendations are a great way of building a customer base. Think about it: how many times have you bought something or visited a new restaurant because a friend or family member told you how good it was? You need to make your brand come alive so that everyone you sell your product or service to becomes a brand ambassador. It's a good idea to get current clients to write testimonials or even have a phone call with potential new clients.

Think about the following methods of marketing your business without putting a finger on your computer.

■ Host a launch event so that you can invite potential customers to meet you.

■ Use customer loyalty cards; if a customer buys five coffees, why not give them a sixth for free?

■ Give discounts to customers that recommend friends and family.

■ Offer free testers or trials of your product, or a free trial of your service for thirty days.

Marketing materials and collateral

So, you've got your brand sorted, your logo has been designed and road-tested and you're itching to bring it all to life so you can start marketing your business. It's all too easy to go crazy at the printers at this stage. Review the marketing section of your business plan before you start sticking your logo on pens, cups and T-shirts! If you're running an online business, it's likely that most of your marketing materials will be digital. If you're setting up a shop, you'll need printed collateral such as bags, sale signs and window posters.

Depending on how much budget you have, you might commission a designer to create collateral for you. Every business will need different materials to launch, but as a start you should look into getting some business cards printed and create a website.

Don't go collateral crazy

To avoid going overboard designing materials or buying stock at the printers, make a list of the marketing materials you think you need, the quantity and cost, and note how they'll promote your business effectively. Remember to note the total cost as you'll need to make sure you have enough budgeted in your cash flow (see Step 5 for cash flow planning) and don't forget that boxes take up a lot of space. Think about where you'll store all of your materials and how you'll transport them to events or meetings.

Sounding Pro: Marketing materials for a gym			
Item	Quantity	Total cost	Usage
Posters	500	£150.00	I'll need posters to put in the windows of local shops to promote the launch event.
A5 Flyers	5,000	£200.00	I'll put flyers through letterboxes in the area we're setting up to drum up some sales.
Business cards	1,000	£75.00	I'll be attending at least two networking events each week, so I'll need cards to exchange details with people.
Pens	1,000	£350.00	I can give away pens to everyone that buys one of our classes or a membership.
USBs or CDs	60	£150.00	The first 60 people to visit will get a fitness plan to take away.
Total	Approx. 12 small boxes	£925.00	

Getting your business cards right

You'll be out and about meeting people and they'll hopefully want to make contact with you to find out more about what you're selling. Your business card is the first brand experience they will have, so think wisely about what your card says and make sure your contact details are clear and – most importantly – correct! Just think how bad you'd feel if you gave away hundreds of cards and realized your email address was wrong so no one could contact you. You'll also need to give yourself a job title that explains who you are in the business. It's worth avoiding just having 'entrepreneur' as it doesn't tell anyone what position you hold. Your card should have the following information:

- your full name
- your role or position, for example, Sales director, CEO, Head chef, Engineer
- telephone number
- email address
- website url

You might also consider adding links to social media profiles such as Twitter or LinkedIn®.

Petersfield Projects

pp

Tony Fawkes M.A.
Managing Director

Petersfield Projects
6 Manor Drive, Petersfield, Sussex PO3 2PZ

T   01377 201564
M 097015 400400
E   tony.fawkes@petersfieldprojects.co.uk
W www.petersfieldprojects.co.uk

Key take-aways

Think about the things you will take away from Step 3 and how you will implement them.

Topic	Take-away	Implementation
Identifying the personality of your business	• *Understand what words describe the brand I am trying to create.* • *Think about how I want people to feel about my business.*	• *Ask family and friends to help me to brainstorm words that they associate with my brand.* • *Review other companies to see how they make their brand come to life.*
Creating a logo		
Creating a strapline		
Managing trademarks and copyright		
Building a website		
Using social media for your business		
Using social media for you		
Using blogs and apps		
Using content platforms		
Marketing your business offline		
Getting your business card right		

Step 4

SELL YOUR PRODUCT OR SERVICE

"Never allow a person to tell you "no" who doesn't have the power to say "yes".' — Eleanor Roosevelt, First Lady of the United States (1884–1962)

Five ways to succeed

Create a simple sales pitch that wows customers.

Understand how to explain your USP.

Research the needs of the people you're selling to.

Pitch your business directly to your customer.

Improve sales continually by asking for feedback.

Five ways to fail

Don't create a sales experience that appeals to customers.

Sound aggressive or desperate during sales calls.

Waste people's time by being unprepared for meetings.

Be defensive if someone highlights a weakness or flaw.

Fail to deliver what you say you will.

The importance of learning to sell

If you want to have a successful business, there's one thing you need to train yourself to be good at: sales. This is the cornerstone of any business.

It's easy to come up with ideas but if you can't figure out who is actually going to buy or benefit from what you're doing, then chances are your business won't make it past the first year. You should have identified during business planning (Step 2) who you're selling to, why they need your product or service and how you're different from your competitors. Knowing these three things will make life a lot easier, whether you're selling direct to consumers (B2C) or to businesses (B2B).

The art of selling

There is an art to selling and it differs depending on your audience. Selling direct to consumers requires an understanding of an individual's motivation to buy. You get this insight through research, consumer focus groups and competitor analysis. Selling to organizations needs big picture thinking; you must consider how your product or service makes the business better or gives it a competitive edge. Review the annual reports of the businesses you're selling to – you can find these on their websites – or industry reviews on Datamonitor.com or Mintel.com. The art of selling is knowing that there are two parts to a sale: the pitch and the sales experience.

The pitch

The pitch happens every time you communicate with potential buyers; it's your thirty-second headline that gets people interested in your product or service. In a retail environment, your pitch might be why a product will make life easier or why it will make someone look or feel great. In a consultancy or service business, the pitch is likely to be related to helping a business to be more productive or profitable, or to increase brand exposure.

The sales experience

The sales experience is all of the non-verbal elements you add to the pitch. It could be the smell and presentation of your freshly baked goods or the 'try before you buy' policy on your new software application.

Selling B2C

If you sell direct to consumers, you should spend some time getting to know their habits. For example, if you open a delicatessen or bakery near a school, it's likely that many of your key customers will be parents doing the school run. This means you might have a busy period after they've dropped their children off at school and another when they're picking them up. Therefore, you might decide to also stock food they could buy as treats for their children. Selling people your products isn't just what comes out of your mouth (although it's good to ask them about their day and be friendly). Selling will be the whole experience: the speed of service, how appealing your food looks and its quality.

It's the same if you're setting up an online boutique; the sales experience doesn't involve just the products. It includes factors such as how easy it is to use the website, whether there is clear guidance on how a pair of trousers or a shirt fits, and how easy it is to check out and pay. The best way to get the sales experience right when selling direct to customers is to put yourself in the position of your customer and think carefully about the experience you want them to have. What would make you say: 'Wow, I'm going back there again', or better yet, recommend it to a friend?

You could also try and speak to your target audience – either in a focus group or one to one on the street – to find out why they'd buy from you, and what they expect in terms of service, which will help you to think about your sales positioning.

Selling B2B

The process of selling to a business is slightly more complex than selling direct to consumers. You need to do a lot of research and the average amount of time from your first contact to signing a contract is roughly three months, so you'll need to make sure you're securing enough new business to cover the period between one contract ending and another starting.

There are typically seven stages in the B2B sales process.

1 **Researching your pipeline:** Your pipeline is the list of potential customers you can sell your product or service to.

2 **Securing the meeting:** You should aim to secure a meeting in the diary or schedule dates to showcase your products to potential buyers.

3 **Pitching for business:** The pitch is where you showcase and sell your product or service to a new customer. Once you secure a sale, you're on track to making your business work.

4 **Closing the deal:** You should aim to close the deal either during the pitch or directly afterwards to save you having to chase clients months after the meeting has taken place.

5 **Delivering on the order:** Once contracts are exchanged or goods are paid for, you deliver the product.

6 **Reviewing quality and customer service:** You should review the quality of service and get client feedback.

7 **Up-selling:** Use your feedback as an opportunity to sell more to your customer (up-selling) or to add new products and services to the offer for existing clients.

Researching your pipeline

Let's discuss this point in more detail. Some of the potential customers on your list will be 'cold' contacts – contacts you don't know or haven't met. You should also have some 'warm' contacts – these might be people that have contacted you directly because they saw some of your marketing materials or you might have been introduced to through friends or your network. They'll be 'warm' because they are open to speaking to you further.

Equally, you may have met someone at a tradeshow (see page 73) or networking event and they've asked to meet you to find out more about you and your business.

To create a pipeline, you need to research:

■ businesses that may want to buy what you're selling.

■ why businesses need what you're selling; essentially, this is your USP, which you will have identified during the business planning phase.

■ the relevant department and a contact name – ideally someone with the power to say 'yes' to buying from you, i.e. a budget holder. You may not know whether someone is a budget holder until you speak to them but heads of departments are a good start.

■ your contact's email address and telephone number. You can usually find this information by searching on the internet or by calling the company reception desk.

Securing the meeting

Once you have your pipeline information, you can begin setting up some meetings. Start with an email introduction and then follow up with a call. If you want to do something that stands out, send your potential customer product samples or offer a free service trial immediately after your introductory email.

The introductory email

Getting your introductory email right will help to secure an initial call or meeting. Your emails should aim to grab the reader's attention and get them interested. They shouldn't be too long, however; 150–200 words is ideal. The key points of your email should be:

■ **a short introduction.**

Start the email with a brief introduction of yourself and your business.

■ **your reason for writing.**

Secondly, state your reason for making contact. Highlight why your product or service will be of benefit to them.

■ **evidence to support your claims.**

Note any feedback you've had from research, focus groups or clients, and any figures such as an increase in subscriptions or sales that either you or your clients have had. In this way, you're showing that what you do works and that you're in demand.

■ **the ask.**

Close the email with the ask: what do you want? A call, a Skype, a meeting? Make it clear.

Cold calling

Unless you've worked in the sales industry, cold calling might be your worst nightmare. Don't worry; you're not alone. However, it's an essential part of making your business a roaring success (because it leads to that all-important sale). It's worth practising your technique with a friend first to check that you can clearly articulate your point over the phone and you don't speak too fast. One trick some people use is to have a picture of the person they're speaking to on the screen in front of them. It helps to humanize the call. You can usually find pictures on LinkedIn® or on the company website. Typical questions you might be asked or objections you might hear are: 'I already have a supplier. Why should I buy from you?' 'How much will your service or product cost to roll out?' 'Who have you worked with previously?'

If you don't have any clients, you'll need to be honest, but you should have tested your concept so you can tell the person you're speaking to about the feedback you've had and who's on your list of potential customers. If the person hears that you're also contacting their competitors, they might want to secure you first.

It's unlikely you'll get a 'Yes, I'll buy that right now' over the phone. You should also remember that people are busy and you may have interrupted their day, so be precise, know what you want to say and try to conclude with a mutually agreed outcome from the call beyond a quick sale. An outcome might be a follow-up call via Skype, a meeting, or twenty minutes to show them your product at an event or trade show you're both attending.

Trade shows and pop-up events

To get a list of 'warm' contacts from day one, you could launch your product or service at a trade show or through a pop-up event.

Trade shows are industry-run events where suppliers and buyers come together to review trends, buy and sell, and make new contacts. Do an internet search to find the best ones for you based on the industry you operate in. Once you have a list of events, the next thing you need to consider is cost. The cost of a stand at a trade show can vary between a few hundred pounds and several thousand. The more exclusive the event, the more expensive it will be. If you're selling luxury goods, it might be worth attending one of the more expensive events to get to meet the buyers from the companies you want to sell to. You'll get to show them your product and schedule time to meet them one on one.

Pop-up events are a relatively new way of selling products. The basic idea is that, through an estate agent or landlord, you find a vacant space with good passing trade and set up a shop, café or restaurant for a short period of time; a week is ideal. You should dress the space to help showcase your brand and products, and the goal is to create opportunities to sell direct to buyers or the local community. Not only do you get yourself some free PR, you create a market for yourself and sell some of your products.

Pitching for business

Preparing for your presentation

So, you've been invited in for a meeting. Even if you're not asked to give a visual presentation, you should be prepared to present both your product or service and yourself.

In order to prepare mentally, you should find out as much as you can about who you'll be meeting. Search for them on Google, Twitter and LinkedIn®. You should check if they've written any articles or spoken at any events to see if they have a position on something you're selling or if they're passionate about a specific part of their industry. You should know what makes them tick and use it in your presentation to show that you understand their needs and the ambitions of their organization. There might be more than one person attending; if so, try and get their names and do some background research on them too.

If you're presenting a product, bring it along in a branded box or bag so it looks professional. If you're explaining your service, use some visuals or have a demo to hand. The key here is to make the meeting as interesting as possible, so keep your energy up and everyone focused on what you're selling. Put yourself in their shoes: what would keep you awake and engaged during a sales meeting?

The pitch

Next, you need to get ready to sing the praises of your product or service from the rooftops with energy and zeal.

You should start the meeting with handshakes all round and introduce yourself and your business again. If appropriate, ask the people present how they are (with sincerity), and if you've seen them doing a talk, refer to it or highlight that you liked something they said in an article. If they haven't done either, refer to a point from a recent company press statement. What you're showing here is that you've done your background research.

Once you're seated, thank them for their time and go straight into your pitch. Explain:

- ■ what you do.

- ■ why you do it.

- ■ how you'll make their life easier and their business better or more profitable.

- ■ who you've worked with previously – to show off your credentials (if relevant).

Keep this bit to less than fifteen minutes and check your speed. Too fast and they'll miss important information. Too slow and you risk sending them to sleep. As discussed, if possible, show your product or highlight the benefits of your service in a visual format to keep your audience engaged and interested, and then open up the presentation for questions.

Going in alone

If you're going into a meeting alone but there are more than two people in the room, you'll need to match their energy or bring along samples or a visual presentation to ensure you have their attention. You want to avoid having three people throwing questions at you or interrupting you because they're bored. Worse still, if you lose them to emails on their phone, it's likely they'll put you off your flow.

Going in with a team

Going in with a team when presenting to more than one person is ideal as you have colleagues that can make eye contact while you're focusing on slides or explaining how your product works. You need to avoid your team talking over you or too many people answering questions, so practise your pitch and be clear about which areas each person will be focusing on before you go in.

Dealing with different personality types

A little trick seasoned sales people use is personality profiling. A useful model for pitching is to follow *Learning Styles Helper's Guide* (2009, Peter Honey and Alan Mumford). In this publication Honey and Mumford proposed the theory that people process information in one of four different ways. It's invaluable in a pitch as you can tailor your responses and delivery to ensure everyone in the room is fully engaged. The basic characteristics of the four main types are as follows:

■ **Activists**

Activists tend to be extroverted and enjoy big picture thinking. In a meeting they'll be very animated and ask lots of questions about why your product or service is so great or better than everything else on the market. They will expect an ambitious and strategic response, and details bore them. Prepare a model of what their business looks like without your help and then what it will be like with your input. Highlighting a positive change will appeal to them.

■ **Pragmatists**

Pragmatists will be focused on the how – they ask questions like 'How will this make our business better?' and 'How soon can you deliver?' They understand the big picture but need to know you can get the job done and that you aren't just promising but then under-deliver. If you have a 'how' person in the room, chances are they are a pragmatist. Make sure you can explain how you plan to deliver your product or service on time and to budget.

■ Theorists

Theorists will be the people in the meeting who ask 'why' questions like 'Why will consumers like your product more than your competitors'?' and 'Why do you think the research suggested the trend for buying mobiles over computers will increase?' They like detail and will buy from you if you can satisfy their need to understand the facts behind your pitch. Give them sales projections or trend forecasts from your research that show why they need you.

■ Reflectors

Reflectors will be the quietest people at the meeting, or if you are seeing them one on one, they'll let you talk and lead the conversation. They will be processing what you say in detail and will ask questions about something you mentioned five or ten minutes before. It's taken them that long to think about it, which means they have no idea what you said after that thought popped into their head. You'll be able to spot them as they'll look uninterested and will probably be looking away (out of a window or over your shoulder) while you're talking. To keep them engaged, ask them questions instead of going through a long monologue and give them samples or visuals to review.

Train yourself to look out for specific words or behaviours so you can identify the profiles of the people you meet with and respond to them effectively. This is especially important if pitching and face-to-face sales are a big part of how your business is going to grow.

Addressing objections

At some point during your pitch, or while trying to sell your product to a customer, you'll come up against an objection or two. Be prepared for this because you'll need to know your stuff inside out to confidently address any concerns. The first time you get an objection you might not know how to answer, but make a note of it because the same objection might come up again, and next time you'll have a better response until your better response becomes a winning response.

There will usually be people in the room who'll make it their job to say 'no'. Remember that 'no' is not an answer. Always regard 'no' as a question: find out what's making the person unsure and consider how you can make them feel more comfortable while giving them the chance to say 'yes' instead. In this situation, you might need to change your language slightly, show sales projections or highlight the positive change that working with you will bring to their business.

This is where giving free trials or getting existing clients to give a testimonial or have a phone call with prospective clients comes in. The most important thing to remember is not to get aggressive, sarcastic or defensive if someone finds fault with what you do. Addressing objections is part of the learning process; use the opportunity to improve your product or service as well as your pitch. And if the same objection comes up time and time again, you probably should take a serious look at your product or service.

Closing the deal

Once you've presented your product or service and won over everyone in the room, shop or trade show by addressing their concerns, you'll need to close the sale. This is the part where you do three things.

■ You must re-confirm what you'll be delivering to your customers. Remember: don't promise anything you know you can't deliver. For example, if you say you'll get them 100 shirts a week for three months, you must do so. And if you say you'll deliver a bouquet of flowers at 8 a.m. on a Saturday, be outside their house at 7.59 a.m. If you fail to deliver, you risk damaging your credibility and you may not get a second chance to prove yourself.

■ For B2B sales, confirm a budget or the price range you're working with (refer back to your figures in Step 2). If you've been asked to go away and come back with a price, aim to give them a benchmark of what the costs might be – it's always good to gauge their reaction in person so that you know if the costs are too high or are close to the amount they're willing to pay.

■ Confirm next steps and a timeline. You need to make sure they know when they can expect to hear from you again and when you will be able to deliver for them. This stops further negotiations dragging on for months. For B2C sales, the same applies: deliver in good time. And if you run a website, for example, which states that your delivery times are two business days, don't leave your customers waiting a week.

Sounding Pro: The pitch

There's a lot to remember when pitching, but practice makes perfect, so here are a few tips on how to make sure the meeting goes smoothly.

Opening the meeting	*Hello (Sam), I'm (Jenny Hart) from (Data Dynamics). Thanks for taking the time to meet with me. I saw your article on the importance of good data systems, so I'm sure you'll like what we're offering.*
Selling the benefits of your product or service (your USP)	*(Data Dynamics) will help you to review and understand all of your customers' buying habits and data so that you can select specific items for them to buy as they go through your website. This will help you to increase your sales by 30% in three months and we're the only company specializing in tracking data in this way.*
Dealing with objections or difficult questions	*I understand that you're not in a position to buy today, so how about a free trial?*
	Is there anything I can do to help you to understand our product better?
	Would you like to speak to some of our other clients? They'll tell you how much we've helped them.
Closing the deal	*To confirm, you'd like to start with a three-month trial.*
	You have a budget of between £2,500 and £3,000 per month.
	Following the trial, we'll have a follow-up meeting to review how it's worked for you.

Delivering on the order

Great customer service is part of the sales process and experience. You should aim to keep selling to your customers and clients, so it's worth investing the time to get the actual delivery of your product or service right. From the packaging of a pair of shoes to the online helpdesk for a new software product, the customer should feel like you care about their business so that they'll keep coming back. Think about what you can do to keep your customers and clients happy and loyal to you. As a top line they'll expect quality, value for money (note that this doesn't necessarily mean cheap) and great service. All of which equals a great sales experience.

Reviewing quality and customer service

To keep your business growing, you should take the time to refine your sales pitch and the sales experience you want to create for your customers.

■ Ask for feedback after pitches, especially if you were unsuccessful in securing a deal. Send follow-up emails asking how you could have done better.

■ Once you've built up a customer or client base, you should ask them to write testimonials or help with referrals. The majority of clients will be happy to do so.

Up-selling

The final stage of the sales process is up-selling and getting repeat business. It's not always necessary to go after new customers or clients. You should think about what else you could sell on the spot (up-selling), for example, a bag with a pair of shoes, or at another point in the year (repeat business), for example, an upgrade on a software contract to keep your business growing. Having a core group of people that buy from you also helps with cash flow planning in the long term because you can factor them into your budgets with confidence.

Key take-aways

Think about the things you will take away from Step 4 and how you will implement them.

Topic	Take-away	Implementation
The importance of learning to sell	• *Sales are an important part of running a successful business.* • *Knowing why someone would buy my product and how it makes their business better is important.*	• *Train myself to be successful at selling my ideas.* • *Research why anyone would want to buy from me and use that information to my advantage.*
The art of selling		
Researching your pipeline		
Securing a sales meeting		
Preparing for a sales pitch		
Delivering a sales pitch		
Dealing with different personalities in a sales pitch		
Addressing objections in a sales pitch		
Closing a deal		
Delivering on the order		
Improving the sales experience		

SET UP YOUR OFFICE AND STAFF

'Deciding what not to do is as important as deciding what to do.' — Steve Jobs, Founder of Apple Inc. (1955–2011)

Five ways to succeed

Put operational processes in place to manage daily tasks.

Organize contacts so you know who you're working with.

Manage your cash flow effectively.

Prepare clear job descriptions for all employees.

Set SMART targets for your teams.

Five ways to fail

Ignore the need to be organized.

Forget to take out business insurance.

Leave taking on an accountant to the last minute.

Employ staff without planning first.

Belittle staff members.

Running your business

So, you've motored along with your business plan, created a brand and started your marketing drive. Your first sales are starting to come through and you'll be thinking about putting some systems and processes in place to make sure the business runs smoothly. You might even be thinking about taking on a member of staff. You might be feeling slightly overwhelmed if not enthused by it all, which means you've reached the point where you should start putting in operational processes like client-relationship management systems (CRM) and invoicing and supply chain management. Ask yourself the following questions and keep them in mind as you read through this step.

■ How will you track the progress of your sales calls?

■ How are you planning to manage your suppliers or track delivery of goods and services to clients?

■ Do you need to take on staff to help out at busy times of the day, week or year?

■ Will you be managing the finances each day or working with a bookkeeper or accountant?

■ Will you be issuing invoices? If so, what information will you include?

■ How will you track when invoices have been submitted and paid?

Managing your contacts

One of two things will happen for you to know it's time to set up your contacts on a database or client-relationship management (CRM) system: you'll either have stacks of business cards on your desk or, even worse, you'll start giving out other people's business cards because there are so many in your wallet. Ideally, take the time to add your contacts to either an Excel spreadsheet or an online CRM system before this happens. If you get into the habit of doing this now, when the time comes to follow up with clients or send off deliveries, you'll be able to access everyone's details easily.

CRM systems and tools to track sales progress

Once you've started building a potential client and customer base, you'll need to manage all of your contacts and keep track of where you've got to with each sale. If you're running a B2B business, this is doubly important as you'll need to follow up with contacts for sales opportunities. There are some great tools on the market that will help you to track contact details, the last time you emailed and called a client, their response, and any follow-up that needs to happen. Have a look at the following websites to see what's on offer and what might work for you.

- www.salesforce.com
- www.insideview.com
- https://highrisehq.com
- www.salespod.net

Managing your money

Good money management will help you both to maintain your business and grow it. This is because a profitable business can still fail if it doesn't have money to pay for the day-to-day operational costs. It's important to set up processes to help you to keep track of everyone you're working with, when they should be delivering to you, how much money you owe them and when you're due to pay.

Having these processes in place makes planning your cash flow – the flow of money in and out of your account on any given day – easier as you know *when* money is coming into and going out of the business. There are lots of free and low-cost ways of tracking your business's money. In the early stages, it's worth being hands-on with the finances so you know and understand the ins and outs of making your business run both effectively and efficiently. For accessible cloud-based (i.e. available online wherever you are) bookkeeping, supplier tracking and issuing of invoices, have a look at xero.com or KashFlow.com. Software solutions such as Sage™, Sage 50 or QuickBooks® are useful if you want an integrated sales, employee payment and invoicing system. There are a number of useful forums detailing how to get the most out of Sage™ and QuickBooks® on Intuit.com.

Cash flow

Cash flow is usually planned on a month-by-month basis. You could also forecast your cash flow twelve months into the future based on work you think you might get or sales you predict you'll make. Having forecasted targets will help you to plan when you need to be selling and closing deals. All cash flow plans should include the following:

■ **Cash *into* the business**

This is the amount of money coming into the business each month. It might come from product sales, subscriptions, loans, investment or contract payments.

■ **Cash *out* of the business**

This is all of the business expenses incurred per month. It will include your salary, staff or freelancer costs, delivery costs, rent, value added tax (VAT), utility bills, travel, marketing and website maintenance.

The figure that you'll want to keep an eye on is the 'cash position', which is how much money you actually have once money out is deducted from the money coming in. Scheduling time each month to review your finances is a good habit. You should try to have more money coming in than going out to keep your business running effectively. Keep track of all of your expenses on a weekly basis so you know your outgoings, and try to save a percentage of your income (twenty per cent is a good benchmark) for unexpected costs.

There are some great free cash flow templates available on Microsoft Office or Mac Numbers, so all you need are the numbers as opposed to creating the template from scratch.

Working with an accountant and bookkeeper

Managing money can be a complex operation, especially if you have to pay staff and issue invoices and receipts to clients.

Accountants

To help you navigate the compliance and regulatory practices that businesses must adhere to, for example, paying VAT on sales, you should work with an accountant. Accountants are professional money managers and they understand how to effectively manage the money going in and out of your business so your cash flow stays healthy. Most accountants offer start-up services such as processing your personal and staff payroll, managing VAT returns and tax returns. To find accountants near you, you can search online, via LinkedIn® and Twitter. If you're in the UK, www.taxassist.co.uk has a list of small business accountancy specialists.

Bookkeepers

Accountants usually support your business with the compliance aspect of money management. However, if you're looking for day-to-day support and logging of receipts and payments, you should look to secure the services of a bookkeeper. Bookkeepers will have trained in the management of credits and debits (money in and out). In the UK, the Institute of Chartered Bookkeepers has a list of all the chartered bookkeepers in the country and is a good place to start looking for one.

Once you have an accountant and bookkeeper on board, they'll be able to review your money management processes and suggest ways to make things easier for you. They'll also have good working knowledge of accounting tools like Xero and Sage®, as previously mentioned.

Invoicing

Invoices are the documents you issue to clients and customers so they can pay you for your products or services. Invoicing is usually only needed for B2B transactions. In B2C sales, you usually only issue receipts for the goods customers have already paid for.

The finance departments of the businesses you work with need specific information in order to process invoices through their systems. So it's important to include all the correct information on your invoices to avoid problems and ensure you're paid on time. Schedule regular times in your diary, maybe fortnightly, to review your invoices and payment dates, and call the finance departments to confirm when invoices will be paid. That way you'll know when to expect money to be paid into your account and when you can schedule to make payments yourself.

When you sign a new contract with a client, review their payment terms to see when they contractually pay their suppliers. Some businesses will pay on the date you stipulate, while others have thirty- to ninety-day payment terms. Bear in mind that this usually refers to business working days, so if a client has a ninety-day payment term, try to negotiate this down. If you're a small business, it's unlikely you'll be able to deliver products or services and then wait for over four months to be paid. It's something that causes a number of new businesses to fail.

Your client will then issue you with a supplier number, which you should include on all your invoices. They may also issue you a purchase order (PO) – a payment registration number that confirms your invoice has been logged on their system. Large businesses and corporations will usually issue a PO number before you can issue them an invoice for payment.

You can find invoice templates online and Microsoft Word and Mac Pages have a template set-up function. Alternatively, you can follow the template below.

Invoice

Data Dynamics
6 Grove Park
Manchester, M2 3LA

Attention: Finance Department
Systems Tech Ltd
123 Belgrave Street
London, N1 3RB

Supplier no: 84521
Product description: 2-month subscription to software
Purchase order: 345123F

January fees	£800.00
February fees	£800.00
Total	£1,600.00
Total (inc VAT)	**£1,920.00**

Payment details:
Derbyshire Bank
Sort code: 12-34-56
Account number: 987654321

Company Registration number: 1234567   Vat number: 23456789
Registered address: Suite 10, Longdown Drive, Lancaster, LA1 2BZ

Note: Make sure you highlight the product or service being paid for on the invoice. If you're registered for VAT, you'll need to add your registration number and the total including VAT separately.

Insurance

It's beneficial to have insurance in place to protect yourself and your business should something unexpected happen. There's some insurance that you'll be legally obligated to have. This varies from country to country or even state to state but for the most part, you'll be expected to have insurance if you have employees and premises that customers and clients visit. Also, if you're offering advice to businesses, you'll need some form of professional indemnity, which means you'll be covered should you advise a business incorrectly and they lose money, or if your advice harms their brand.

In the UK, you need to have the following insurances.

■ **Employer's liability**

This covers you should anything happen to your employees, for example, they fall off a ladder stacking a shelf or they cut themselves badly preparing food.

■ **Public liability**

This covers you should anything happen to anyone that is not an employee while they are on your premises, for example, they fall on your shop floor while shopping.

■ **Professional indemnity**

This insurance is primarily for consultancies and service-based businesses. It covers you against claims should you give bad advice or guidance that damages a client's brand or operations.

An internet search will list a number of business insurance providers, and most mainstream commercial brands offer a small business package.

Managing your supply chain

Setting up retail-tracking processes

If you're running a retail business, there will be operational tasks that you have to do daily, such as refilling stock on shelves or tracking new deliveries to your warehouse. In a restaurant, bakery or café, your suppliers and supply chain would be all of the people that bring your cooking supplies or your packaging for take-away orders.

If you want to track stock in a shop or online, investing in a good electronic point of sale (EPoS) system is key. EPoS systems are smart databases of all of your products; when you sell something, your inventory list is updated so you can see what's been sold and when. EPoS systems vary greatly depending on the business you run, so do an internet search and give the companies a call to discuss your requirements.

Planning for your staffing needs

There is really only one thing that will help you to decide on your future staffing needs: the amount of work that needs to be done. You can base your estimate for this on the orders you've already received and your sales forecast (see Step 2). This will enable you to predict future production levels and therefore staffing requirements for the short, medium and long term. For example, imagine you've forecast a thirty per cent increase in sales in the next six months and this is based on selling an additional 700 products or servicing an additional five clients. Now you have to consider how many staff you need and what level of expertise they must have in order to deliver the products or services. Once you've established this, you can begin to budget for recruiting and employing staff. Use the checklist below to make sure you don't forget anything.

Sounding Pro: Employment planning and costing

	Budgeted cost
Recruitment process, including advertising or agency fees	
Induction or training required	
Salary, employer tax	
Additional equipment, e.g. computer, desk, telephone, car	
Any obligatory pension contributions or other benefits you are legally obliged to provide in the country where you operate your business	
Insurance	
The value of your time spent recruiting, training, inducting, etc.	
Total	

Something to consider before beginning the recruitment process is whether you need to employ full- or part-time permanent staff, or whether there are other options for your business.

Casual or temporary staff

If your business is seasonal, such as farm work or something related to summer tourism, you may wish to consider casual or temporary staff. You won't incur the long-term financial commitment when the work runs out over the winter months and you won't be required to give them paid holiday or sick leave. On the other hand, there may not be much staff loyalty and you can expect a high staff turnover as people move on to more permanent positions. There are agencies in most big towns and cities that can help source this type of staff.

Freelancers and contractors

If you wish to hire in skilled expertise for the short term or on an ad hoc basis, such as a PR expert to work on a one-off PR campaign, or a graphic designer to provide design work for a client project, you might wish to consider a freelancer or contractor. Generally, these people will be self-employed or running their own business and they will be responsible for their own income tax liabilities. You may agree a fixed price for a piece of work or a rate based upon days or hours worked; either way, you won't be liable for paid holiday or sick leave, or any other benefits that need to be offered to permanent employed staff. To find a contractor or freelancer, there are specialist websites: www.freelancer.co.uk, www.peopleperhour.com or www.elance.com. Alternatively, LinkedIn® is becoming a very popular tool to search for contractors, enabling you to do some research on them before making initial contact.

Interns

An intern will usually be a university graduate who is interested in gaining work experience and skills. In the UK, an intern will generally be entitled to the minimum wage unless they're working for a charity or other not-for-profit organization. Depending on your business and sector, an intern could be an eager and cheap, short-term solution if you're looking for casual or temporary staff. However, you must provide them with the opportunity to learn through their work. Contact your local universities to find out if you can directly source interns through them or sign up to a scheme such as www.inspiringinterns.com or graduatetalentpool.bis.gov.uk.

Apprentices

If your business requires skilled labour, you may wish to consider an apprentice, usually a young person or school- or college-leaver. Apprenticeship schemes incorporate work and the chance to gain skills and a qualification. Many countries, including the UK, run government-backed apprenticeship schemes which offer financial support and promotion to companies registering with them. If your business is in the UK, refer to www.apprenticeships.org.uk.

Employing the right people

Employing the best people for the job is really important for the performance of your business and its reputation. Don't rush to take on the first person you see because you're desperate to fill a position.

The job description

The first step in getting the best people for the job is to put together a good job description. Start by outlining the purpose of the role with the key duties and expectations. List the essential skills, experience and qualifications required in order to fill the position first, and then list those that are desirable but not essential.

Don't forget to include information on the core competencies required, such as *team player* or *self-starter*. This will help potential applicants to evaluate whether the job would suit them and in turn enable you to probe into these areas further at interview stage. You may also wish to include information about the culture of your business and any values that you hold. For instance, if you want your business to be perceived as vibrant and dynamic, make this clear. Be honest and clear with the information you include in the job description and you will be more likely to find the right person, someone who will stay for the long term and make a positive contribution to the business. A good salary and benefits, with training and development opportunities will also be a factor for potential employees, but your budget will be the deciding factor for what you can offer. Look at similar jobs being advertised in your area and establish what the going rate is for the type of position you are offering.

The selection process

You might think that choosing a suitable candidate is as simple as interviewing a number of people and then making a decision, but you need to put effort into selecting a candidate so that you end up with the best person for the job. Make sure you compile a set of relevant open-ended questions to ask during interviews, which require the candidates to discuss their previous experience in detail and describe how they handled situations that are likely to come up in your business. Be consistent and ask each candidate the same set of questions. If you have specific questions that relate to the candidate's experience, ask them, but generally it's best practice to ask the same questions of each of the candidates so that you can compare their experience and skills easily.

Test your candidates at a level appropriate to the position and where possible, prepare tests based on real business scenarios. For example, if you're looking for a telephone sales operator, ask candidates to do a role-play with you acting as the potential customer. Or you may need a qualified project manager and want to test candidates' organizational skills in a written exercise. Assessments like this will give you a good idea of how people work under pressure and their levels of ability. Remember: you're not trying to catch them out; you're looking for supporting evidence that they can perform the required duties.

Do shortlist the suitable candidates and invite them back for a second interview. You may discover new things about them which weren't revealed during your first meeting. Finally, always ask for references and don't forget to follow these up.

Managing and motivating people

You may think that once you've taken on new staff they'll just get on with the job, but that's not the case. Managing people is a task in itself and it shouldn't be underestimated. That's not to say that it can't be enjoyable, especially once good working relationships have been developed.

The ideal situation is for you to spend less time on managing people and more time on the business, but in a small business it's unlikely that you'll ever be able to delegate this task completely. Also, it's probably not a good idea to do so as you need to know how your staff are feeling and performing. Once they are trained and inducted into the business and the job, it's important to specify and clarify your expectations. Consider the objectives or key performance indicators (KPIs) you wish to set your staff. Be sure to make all of their objectives SMART, in other words:

- **S**pecific: State exactly what you want them to achieve.

- **M**easurable: Define the quality or quantity of the objective.

- **A**chievable: Objectives should stretch them but they shouldn't be unrealistic.

- **R**ealistic: Do you have the resources or employees required to achieve an objective and is the objective realistic in the current market?

- **T**ime-specific: Be clear about the timescale within which objectives need to be achieved.

How to get the best out of people

We human beings are a complex lot and we all have unique personalities, needs and wants. It's worth getting to know your staff well and understanding what drives them so that, where possible, you can ensure that their position enables them to use elements of what they enjoy doing in order to get the best out of them. It's a good idea to put processes in place that review the progress your staff are making. You could request weekly or monthly update reports and regular review meetings, along with a more formal review at agreed times, for example, one every six months or annually. This will enable you to keep track of your staff's workloads, spot any potential problems before they happen, and evaluate if someone is ready to step up to the next level or is struggling.

It's also important to keep your staff motivated and there are incentives that help to achieve this. Typically, people want more money, longer holidays or other benefits but this may not be possible. However, if they enjoy their work and like the people they work with and the company they work for, they're more likely to remain motivated and stay, and become an asset to the organization.

So, how can you motivate your staff?

Give praise for a job well done. This sounds obvious but it's often forgotten. But it's easy to do and goes a long way toward making people feel good and appreciated.

Trust your staff to make decisions for themselves. This might lead to the odd mistake but it will help them to learn to become more competent and to handle more responsibility.

Develop a 'no-blame' culture. Negative criticism is demotivating and may cause resentment and disempowerment. Instead, analyse why something went wrong, offer constructive feedback and put processes in place to stop the mistake from being repeated.

Communicate effectively. This means listening as well as talking. Create opportunities for your staff to feed in their ideas and keep them involved in the company's plans as much as you can.

Give them purpose. We all need to understand why we're doing something and to feel that what we do has purpose. Be clear on how their role contributes to the company's mission.

Ask for solutions to problems. You could provide all of the answers yourself but if you ask your staff to come to meetings with solutions to problems, you'll encourage them to be innovative and you won't have to be the sole problem solver in the organization.

Provide good coffee. OK, this is a bit of a strange one but people often get more frustrated about the little day-to-day things in their work environment than anything else. Think about what you can offer that won't break the bank, and keep all facilities well-maintained.

Key take-aways

Think about the things you will take away from Step 5 and how you will implement them.

Topic	Take-away	Implementation
The importance of managing business operations efficiently	• *Managing the operations of my business will help my business to be more efficient.* • *Planning which processes I need is important and will help my business to grow.*	• *Schedule time in my diary to carry out operational tasks.* • *Set up systems to manage contacts and invoicing.*
Managing contacts		
Managing cash flow		
Working with accountants and bookkeepers		
Setting up invoices		
Managing supply chains		
Planning for staffing needs		
Recruiting		
Managing employees		

Step 6

GROW YOUR BUSINESS

'Running that first shop taught me business is not financial science; it's about trading: buying and selling.' — Dame Anita Roddick, founder of The Body Shop® (1942–2007)

Five ways to succeed

Make your business stable enough to grow.

Grow through new products or markets.

Join an incubator or accelerator programme.

Offer complimentary products and services.

Provide first-class customer service.

Five ways to fail

Plan growth without knowing who your buyers are.

Hire inexperienced staff to manage new operations.

Finance expansion plans without sufficient money.

Expect that all customers want the same things.

Dive feet-first into a new international market.

Why go for growth?

Most big brands you can think of started life as small businesses. Marks and Spencer started as a penny bazaar in Leeds; Richard Branson launched the Virgin Group Ltd. brand with less than £200 pounds in cash, and Facebook was a friendship network for Harvard University students. Over time, you'll want to push the potential of your business to increase both revenue and profits. If you haven't already planned to grow quickly as part of your initial business plan, this is when you should start thinking about growth and planning a strategy to move forward. But before you run off and set up an office overseas, think about why you want to grow and what your eventual goal is. Ask yourself the following questions to help you to navigate this exciting but challenging phase.

- Can I afford to spend time and money planning and executing a growth strategy?

- Do I have the finances available to start growing, or will I need investment?

- Will I be able to find the right team members to help grow the business?

- Do I want to grow by scaling operations where I am, or by starting operations in another country or multiple countries?

Creating a growth strategy

Growing a business is similar to starting up again: you'll need to plan, think about your brand positioning, drive increased sales and hire more staff. Before you commit any time or resources to growing your business, you should develop a strategy to help guide you through each step. Your strategy should assess the potential risks involved in growing your business, such as not having enough staff to manage expansion, not delivering products to customers on time, not having enough money to cover the operational costs of growing, or indeed committing too much money where the financial return might not be good enough. You should also think about the various ways in which you can grow. The first consideration should be 'growing up' versus 'growing out'.

Growing up

A strategy that focuses on 'growing up' looks at selling the *same* products or services but across new markets or industries. You might be selling cycle equipment direct to customers and decide that the time has come to focus some of your business on corporate contracts. Or similarly, your clothing business might expand from selling directly from your shop to selling wholesale through other retailers. You might also take your offering to a new region, country or continent through online sales or by setting up a team on the ground.

Growing out

A 'growing out' strategy is all about selling *new* products and services outside of your current offering but most likely to the same industry or market. If you decide on this strategy, you're probably very comfortable operating in a specific industry and have noticed gaps in the market that new products can fill. For example, if you run a bakery, you might consider launching a new brand of bread or offering classes to people who are keen to learn how to bake at home. If you're considering this as a growth strategy, you'll need to make sure your current product or service is either established in your market, or that your new offering is complementary. If you start spending all of your time pushing something new, your existing business might suffer.

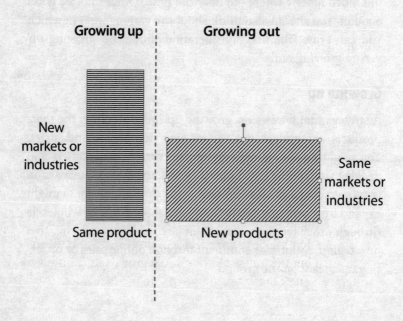

Ways to grow

There are a number of ways to grow a business. The way you choose ultimately depends on the type of business you're running and your ambition for the business in the long term. The case studies at the end of this step highlight how two famous brands scaled their operation over time using two of the methods below.

■ **Organic growth through increased sales and expansion**

This method utilizes the cash already in the business to expand your team so that you can focus on sales and delivery.

■ **Incubation or acceleration**

A popular method in the fast-growth start-up space, incubation or acceleration is where your business is supported by another organization to access funding, to find board members or mentors, or to further develop your launch or growth strategy.

■ **Through investment**

As previously mentioned, securing investment to grow your business is a way of growing quickly without having to save the money first. This option might require you to give away shares in your business.

■ **Targeting new local and global markets and industries**

This option might require a mix of investment and diversification but the premise is that you'll grow your business by targeting new markets or industries to increase sales.

■ **Through diversification or franchising**

While you're running your business, you might come across a new business model or revenue stream that causes you to start up a new business operation. Adding new products and services to your business portfolio will aid growth. You might also consider franchising your business model to other people in a different city or region.

Organic growth

If you have steady sales and big enough profit margins to use your surplus cash to reinvest in the business, you might consider growing your business organically. Organic growth is all about attracting new customers and tracking growth steadily. The reason this kind of growth is called organic is because you fund expansion by reinvesting profits into the business, which requires good cash flow management (see Step 5), a well thought-out sales plan (see Step 4) and experienced staff to manage the increase in work. In most cases, organic growth is linked to expanding your team to maximize sales potential. New hires are usually sales people or, in the case of a consultancy industry, experts or senior talent that your new clients will respect and want to work with.

Attracting new customers

Unless you're going to rely on your existing customer base increasing their orders, the real key to growing your business is attracting new customers, and the areas covered in this step will help you with this task.

Don't forget that there are easy ways to attract new customers. By far the best and cheapest way to do this is by word of mouth and recommendations from existing or previous customers. This also requires the least effort from you ... or does it? Clients will only recommend you if they've received great service at a good price. As long as you consistently offer this, the odd email or letter encouraging your client to recommend you to someone else is absolutely fine. If you know you've provided a good service or quality product and the customer is genuinely happy, don't be shy to ask for a bit of PR from them. Include testimonials and reviews on your website, promotional materials and in advertising.

Use your expertise creatively in the search for new customers, offer to speak at events, such as industry sector conferences, or go to www.ted.com to find out where your local TEDxTalks are taking place and offer to get involved. (TEDxTalks are events where people share their ideas through presentations, which are filmed and uploaded to the TEDx global community on YouTube.) Participate in webinars or write blogs for industry sector or business magazines. Most of the big banks now have online communities offering business advice and they're always looking for businesses to profile. It's a great way of showcasing what you're passionate about, and the more you get involved, the more likely you are to be seen as an expert in your field and attract people to you.

Taking on experienced hires

Part of your growth strategy might be taking on new staff members that are experienced in a specific area you're trying to develop. For example, you might hire a sales or business development director to help you to train your existing sales teams. In a technology business, you might want to take on a chief technology officer (CTO), and some investors might even stipulate this as part of their deal. Or if you're setting up an office elsewhere, you might hire a managing director to lead the operations for one or more of your new sites.

New hires at this level will be expensive; the amount of money you need will depend on the industry and level, but as a guide, review job posts for similar roles and note the salaries offered. You can offer incentives, such as company shares, longer holidays or flexible working if you can't match the salaries others offer. You might also put the opportunity out through your existing contacts to see if they know people looking for a new and exciting challenge.

Incubators and accelerators

Incubators

Now, a slightly different approach to growth that some businesses use is incubation or acceleration. Incubators and accelerators usually support a number of businesses at any one time so that they can launch or grow quickly. They are run by private companies, universities and, in some countries, government agencies.

Incubators are usually for early-stage businesses that have yet to start trading, but the idea behind the business is so good that it warrants support from an incubation centre. These businesses are usually technology- or product-based and they get a mix of support services to help them grow in the early days of starting up. The benefit of this for you might be instant access to funding, new board members, possibly office space and mentors. Some incubators will ask for a share of your business in return or a commission on any investment you raise while they support you.

Accelerators

Accelerators offer the same help and support as incubators, but they focus on businesses that have the potential to secure large amounts of funding quickly or that have possibly launched or developed a prototype already. To get access to an accelerator, your business should be ready for investment from angels or venture capitalists (see Step 1). You'll usually be supported to form a board of directors, find business partners and roll out your product quickly. Again, there is a technology and product bias but there are exceptions. Check out the following incubators and accelerators to see if they can help you.

- www.wayra.org
- www.seedcamp.com
- www.schoolforcreativestartups.com
- www.ycombinator.com
- www.thehot500.co.uk

Employing staff

People are often described as the most valuable asset of a business and they can help your business to grow bigger more quickly. However, recruiting staff is a very big step for any business, and involves legal constraints and financial commitments that must be thought through carefully. You will, of course, have to pay salaries and there will also be additional costs for recruitment, larger premises, furniture, utility bills, insurance, tax, national insurance, pension contributions, sick and holiday leave, and any additional benefits you intend to offer, such as training and extended maternity leave.

When to employ

So, when is a good time to start employing staff? Much will depend on the type and size of your business but if you don't intend to remain a one-man or one-woman band forever, it's something you'll need to think about.

For some businesses, there's no choice but to employ people. For example, if you're setting up a shop or restaurant, you're likely to need other people to work there in addition to yourself. For other businesses, it might be a case of waiting until you have a full order book before taking on staff.

Raising investment for growth

As you grow, you might need to secure money to cover the costs of buying new equipment, launching a new product, hiring experienced team members or setting up another office. If, by doing this, you look likely to become a profitable operation, investors or corporate financers might be interested in helping you to grow. As previously mentioned in Step 1, there are different types of investors and you'll need to work out if a business angel or venture capitalist is right for you at this stage. As a rule of thumb: if you need up to £250,000, you could secure this through angels; for amounts over this, you should explore options for backing by venture capitalists.

If you're considering raising investment, you'll need to work on a new business plan for your growth plan. Follow the template outlined in Step 2, but this time you'll need to include evidence of your actual and current performance and business sales. To add to the overall impact when you're presenting to investors, include client testimonials about how great your product or service is. Also give prospective clients or customers a call to find out if they'd buy the new products or services you're planning to offer. If you can say that your new sales prospects are warm already or if you can highlight why your new product will work for your current clients, it's likely you'll be seen as a viable prospect. If you're working on a new digital offering as part of your growth plan, use examples of how similar sites are faring.

Targeting new markets

Take a good look at your existing market and analyse it as thoroughly as you can. Are you able to work out the demographics of your existing buyers? Now might be a good time to carry out a survey or conduct a focus group with your customers to find out a bit more about them and why they buy your products and services. Once you have this information, think carefully about whether a different group of people may have similar needs or buying habits to your existing customers. Here are some examples.

Product/Service	Existing customers	New market potentials
Vintage wedding dresses	Women aged 35+ living within a 75-mile radius	• Younger women aged 26–34 Consider using younger models and settings for the promotional materials, and also using Google ads. • Women from 75+ miles away Consider working with other local businesses to offer a day package for women coming to try on dresses. We could include a champagne lunch and a manicure or make-up lesson.
Life and executive coaching	• Corporate men and women, aged 27–42 • Women/Men going through a life change, such as having children or getting divorced	Corporate organizations that are making big changes, willing to invest in staff development

Diversification

One way to grow your business is to consider diversifying your product or services by providing new offerings that complement your existing ones. Diversifying can provide you with a number of different sources of income, which can be particularly useful if some of your products or services are seasonal. Here are some examples of diversification.

Existing product/service	Opportunities for diversifying
A café, which sells products to be consumed on the premises	Consider selling take-home complementary products, such as fair trade coffee beans, mugs with your brand and recipe books based on your products.
A marketing consultancy offering services to other businesses	Consider running training courses in marketing for small businesses or college students.
A business designing and selling gift paper and cards, but which relies heavily on the Christmas season to make a small profit	Consider using the designs on new products, such as wallpaper, bags, tea towels and bed linen.
A florist selling to the general public	Consider supplying other local businesses, such as hotels, offices and restaurants with regular displays.

A well-known business that has successfully diversified its product range and developed additional services for its B2B customers, along with a consumer product range is Caterpillar, a leading manufacturer of construction and mining equipment, which now offers finance, maintenance and training, alongside a range of safety and fashion footwear.

Franchising

This is perhaps the most complex area for growth and will not suit all businesses. That said, it can be a very effective growth strategy for some businesses. Some bigger brands that have franchised effectively are KFC (food), Century 21 UK (estate agents), Fit4Less (fitness and leisure) and B&Q (DIY stores).

By franchising your business, you will be granting someone else a licence to trade using your brand and business model for an upfront fee and regular royalties. You'll need to provide them with well-documented earnings potential, a thorough set of guides and structured training on how to run the business, along with detailed information about your brand assets (i.e. how your brand can and can't be used). Franchising can be a great way of introducing investment into your business without the risk of debt and moving into new locations.

Franchising is not something to be undertaken lightly and will only be for you if your business is doing well, has a good track record and is a proven concept. It's not a solution for ailing businesses; if you can't make your business work, how will someone else? You'll need systems and well-documented operating procedures in place so that any franchisee could learn to run the business within a few months. You'll certainly need the expertise of a franchise lawyer but there are also plenty of reputable organizations offering advice, seminars and conferences that can help you. In the UK, for example, these include:

- The British Franchising Association – www.thebfa.org
- International Franchise Association – www.franchise.org
- Franchise Direct UK – www.franchisedirect.co.uk

International expansion

Could your business expand into international markets? Maybe you've already had interest from potential international customers? Some businesses are easier and more likely to expand internationally and this isn't always because of the internet (see page 120 for information about expanding online). Take, for instance, a business that provides translation services, or another that supplies microchips for computers. These two would have an obvious advantage when trading internationally but that's not to say that it's impossible for an organic food and drinks company or a jewellery designer to view the world as a potential marketplace.

International expansion requires careful thought and advice, and it's vital that you understand the cultural and practical differences in the countries you're intending to go into as a lack of knowledge could mean the difference between trading there successfully and not trading at all.

There are organizations that offer assistance to businesses wishing to access international markets and they're a very good place to start if this is something you're considering. Try the Chambers of Commerce, who have offices all over the world, or a trade association relevant to your business. The UK Trade and Investment (www.ukti.gov.uk) is dedicated to helping UK businesses to export and do business overseas.

Below are some areas where these organizations can help.

Culture and religion: Are there specifics about your existing products or services that would need changing to reflect the cultural or religious differences in this new market?

Business practices: How is business done in this marketplace? Is there a specific business etiquette?

Finance and currency: Are you set up to accept foreign currencies? If you're unsure, speak to your bank. Do payment terms differ and can your customers pay electronically?

Overseas distribution and shipping: How will this work and what's the cost? Do you need a distributor within the country to re-sell your products, and how will you find the right one?

Taxes and laws: It's important to be aware of these to ensure that you're trading legally.

Licences: Do you need specific licences for what you want to do?

Your supply chain: How can your potential supply chain be thoroughly checked out, and who can help you to do this? Do the companies you're dealing with hold the correct licences?

Translation services: Where can you find a translator to help?

Expanding online

We discussed the value of having a website and using social media in Step 3, but trading online is another great way to grow your business.

If you don't already do so, could you now sell your product range online? This might mean upgrading your own website to that of an e-commerce site that can offer order fulfilment and accept payment. If this is a route you wish to take, you need to consider which locations you can supply to. If you decide to sell overseas, consider some of the questions on page 119 about trading internationally, specifically those about distribution and shipping and finance and currencies. On your website, be clear about where you will ship goods to, expected delivery times and what the postage and packing costs will be. Depending on how global you decide to go with your sales, you may also want to consider getting your website translated into a number of different languages, perhaps starting with one or two used in territories where you've decided you'd like to grow first.

Using larger, well-known online sales platforms such as eBay™, Amazon or Notonthehighstreet.com can really open up your marketplace and be a great way to test new markets. Typically, these platforms will take a percentage of your sales but they provide access to a much larger potential customer base through their brand awareness and a large marketing budget. They will all have a set of standard terms and conditions, which you should read closely. And be aware that you will not be able to negotiate individual terms or conditions.

Online services

If your business is service- rather than product-based, you might be wondering how online expansion could work for you. Have you thought about offering some of your services online? For instance, if you offer training services, could you package up short online courses and sell them through your site? Or if you offer professional services such as accountancy or law, could you write short guides for existing and new clients? You may decide not to charge for some of your online services but instead use them to enhance your reputation or as a taster to attract new clients.

If your business offers consultancy type services such as fund-raising, IT, design, marketing and environmental, another way to expand with an online presence is by signing up to an approved directory or matching service; this will make your business offering visible to a wider audience. There are plenty of such services available for different sectors, specialisms and locations, whose purpose is to help potential clients to find qualified and trusted consultants. Contact the relevant organizations before signing up to discuss how much work on average a consultant in your line of business could expect from joining, and weigh this up against any fees. Below are some examples of such directories in the UK.

- www.skillfair.co.uk – tenders and projects matching service for consultants

- www.ncvo.org.uk – a directory of approved consultants for the voluntary sector

- www.endsdirectory.com – a listing of environmental consultants and other eco-service providers

- www.designdirectory.co.uk – a directory of design consultants, including fashion, architectural and website

Case studies

To help you understand the various ways you can grow your business, we've chosen two brands and explained how they've grown. They are examples of what it looks like when your business 'grows up' or 'grows out'. Both show how one core product has helped drive business growth and has ultimately brought success. Use the case studies as tools to think about how you can do the same with your product or service.

CrossFit Inc.

CrossFit Inc. was founded by Greg Glassman in 2000. The business model is quite simple: it's a fitness programme that combines body conditioning and strength-based exercises, such as aerobics and Olympic weightlifting. The way the exercises are put together in a class is the USP of the business and that, along with a dedicated group of users, has taken the brand from a local gym class to a global brand. The business has 'grown up' by expanding the core CrossFit workout all over the world. Their product is the same worldwide but growth is driven by trainers setting up gym networks in their own cities. So far, there are 7,000 CrossFit centres and they all work to the same programme. Workouts can also be accessed online, which is another way of growing up without needing to have a physical presence in a new place.

Apple Inc.

Apple Computer Inc. was founded in 1976 by Steve Jobs, Ronald Wayne and Steve Wozniak. The business model was selling computers and computer software, namely the Apple Macintosh, which was later known as the iMac. The company has had its ups and downs over the years but survived long enough to position itself as a market leader in computers for the design and creative industries. This was, in part, due to the strong design principle that went into the development of the computers but also because the software worked so well for producing creative materials.

In 2000 Apple set about 'growing out' and thinking about what new industries they could operate in successfully. In order to do this, they changed their name to Apple Inc. and set about rebranding to a consumer products business. In October 2001 the iPod was launched and nearly overnight revolutionized the music industry. This was followed by the iPhone, which had the same impact on the telecoms industry, and the iPad, which led full circle back to computers. The growth plan for Apple Inc. was all about diversification through new products that were not part of their original business. As a result, the Apple Inc. brand has become known for innovation and a strong design aesthetic.

Your business, product and service could look completely different a couple of years from now. The important thing is to be open: open to opportunities, industries and markets. Then you can decide if growth is right for you once you've explored all of your options.

Key take-aways

Think about the things you will take away from Step 6 and how you will implement them.

Topic	Take-away	Implementation
Creating a growth strategy	• *Consider the impact growing will have on the business.* • *Grow by selling more of the same to different customers or new products to the same customers.*	• *Develop a plan to look at the risks and opportunities of growing the business.* • *Review ideas to grow out or up and decide which would work best.*
Ways to grow		
Growing organically		
Diversifying your range		
Targeting new markets		
Franchising		
Expanding into international markets		
Expanding online		

REVIEW YOUR BUSINESS AND PROGRESS

'As long as you're going to be thinking anyway, think big.' — Donald Trump, business magnate

Five ways to succeed

Define your goals.

Manage your time well.

Widen your network.

Recognize any culture shifts in your business.

Thoroughly research a new mentor or coach.

Five ways to fail

Carry on doing things as you always have.

Network without a purpose.

Stick with the same suppliers.

Meet with a mentor without a plan.

Neglect your personal life.

Taking stock

Starting, running and growing a business requires guts and determination, as you probably know by now. If you've come this far, you should take time to reflect on what you've achieved and, most importantly, give yourself a pat on the back. It's all too easy to speed through the start-up phase; before you know it, you're a year in and you've forgotten to stop and reflect on what you've learnt. If you were an employee, you'd have appraisals from your manager on your performance; taking stock by reflecting is your own personal appraisal and feedback session. Taking stock isn't just about the business. Think for a moment about your personal successes and challenges during the start-up phase of your business. How did you handle setbacks? Did you make time to relax or have you been burning the candle at both ends? Are you rewarding yourself for working hard and staying focused? If you've been pushing yourself without reward, remind yourself just how far you've come. Making time to do this, maybe every six months, will give you bursts of energy when you need it most and you'll also have the benefit of hindsight so that the next time you're faced with a challenge you'll know you can handle it.

It's also a good idea to review progress against your business plan and note what has and hasn't been achieved. Make a list of your successes and failures during this time period. What has worked well and what hasn't? How and where can changes and improvements be made and what have been the key lessons you've learnt?

Reviewing business performance

Schedule time to periodically review how things are going both for the business and for you. Setting up and running your business shouldn't burn you out or leave you feeling anxious. If you're feeling uncertain about anything, it's a good idea to create a checklist, like the one below, of milestones you want to achieve and a plan for how you aim to get to where you want to be.

Target	Achieved?	Action
Four clients by the end of the first year	Yes – we have five clients.	None required
Pipeline of at least three clients at any one time	No	Set up at least two meetings a week with prospective clients and get testimonials or recommendations from current clients.
Turnover of £150,000 by the end of the financial year	No – we undercharged.	Review costs and increase daily rates on the next client project.
Find affordable office space for three people	Yes	None required
Recruit a project support officer	No	Increase turnover so we can afford to take on extra help in the next three months.

Becoming a leader

Now that you've reviewed the performance of your business, you should think about how you can be more effective in your role as leader. It's easy to get bogged down in the day-to-day running of your business, so much so that you end up working *in* your business and not *on* your business. If you're running a bakery, you might consider taking on help to do the morning bake, freeing you up to get the shop ready for customers. Or as a consultant, you might be spending too much time writing up reports, which is valuable time away from securing your next big client. If your to-do list is growing and you're not having much luck getting through essential tasks each day, take a step back and think about what can be started or finished by a temporary member of staff or freelancer. This will mean you've always got time to think about driving your business forward and *leading* development and growth. Leadership is all about having vision and getting clients and your team behind you, so much so that they buy from you and they work hard for you and the business you are trying to build. If you're stuck in a cupboard counting stock, you're not actually doing a vital task, one that should be on your to-do list every day – being the leader. Knowing the difference between spending too much time working in and not on your business, and therefore not leading, can, in some cases, be the difference between success and failure.

Leadership

If you started your business with the dream of becoming the next Richard Branson or Arianna Huffington, you'll need to think about how to become the leader of your business and brand and not just a business owner or manager. Good leadership requires a heightened business skill set, for example, resilience, empathy, creativity and a great deal of self-coaching in order to really understand how to build a great company and a team that follow you because they believe in the vision you're trying to create together.

You can develop these skills through training, mentoring or coaching but they don't come together overnight; they take daily practice and planning. Have a look at some of the leadership articles on the Harvard Business Review website (www.hbr.org) or watch videos on leadership and growing organizations on TEDxTalks (www.ted.com) for inspiration.

Understanding the culture of a business

The culture of a business is determined by the behaviour of the people within it. Culture includes the vision, values, brand, systems, beliefs and working practices. It's the set of beliefs and behaviours that is passed on to new employees. Some businesses are famous for shaping their company culture; for example, Microsoft is known for providing a great family-oriented working environment, and Innocent (the drinks company) is known for its quirky and creative environment, which follows through into the brand.

If you've employed staff, your business is likely to have developed its own culture by now, so it's a good time to take a look at that culture to check whether it fits with the vision, values, personality and identity that you originally intended for it. You don't want a disconnect between your vision and values and the day-to-day culture and working practices developed by your staff.

Do your staff understand the vision you have for your business? Are they clear on its values and do they understand how to use these values in their working life? Ask them to think about what they can do to ensure that they live the brand and the values of the organization. For example, if one of your values is simplicity, are they being as clear and concise as possible in all communications with customers?

Reviewing the effectiveness of your business networks

When starting a business, it's essential to develop your networks (see Step 1). When was the last time you reviewed the effectiveness of those networks? Do you know if they're serving their purpose and working for the business, or have they become part of your comfort zone?

List the networks, for example, customers and suppliers. Ask yourself the following questions about each.

- Do they buy from your business or are they a strong prospect?

- Have they introduced you to other useful contacts or sales prospects?

- Do they supply products or provide another service to your business, for example, information, knowledge, technical help and advice?

If you can't answer 'yes' to any of the above, consider carefully whether you want to keep them in the business network and continue to devote time to them. You may have other or more personal reasons for staying in touch with them, which is absolutely fine, but make a note of these so that you're clear why they're still part of the network.

Once you have edited your list, review it and decide whether you need to add more people to it who can help your business. Think about the type of help you need. For example, can someone introduce you to contacts in a particular business that you'd like to talk to, or is it purely new sales prospects you're looking for? Once you know what areas you need help with, start to list where you might find people who can help you.

Reviewing expenditure

Reviewing your expenditure is important to make your business more efficient. It's a good exercise to perform on an annual basis or when policies are due for renewal. The following are specific areas to consider.

■ **Suppliers:** Have they increased their costs over the time period? Are you still getting value for money? It's worth putting the larger pieces of work out to tender on an annual basis, but still worth looking at the smaller suppliers as well. Of course, it's not all about cost with your suppliers; you will also need to consider the service and quality of any goods. There's a balance.

■ **Insurance:** Don't just automatically renew your annual policies. Shop around to ensure that you're getting the best price for the cover you need.

■ **Utilities for premises:** As with insurance policies, shop around. Heating, electricity, telephones and broadband can be expensive, so keep abreast of what other suppliers can offer.

■ **Banks:** It's too complicated to change your bank regularly but after an initial period for new businesses, many banks increase their charges. Check you're using or need all of the services you're paying for and if you're not happy with the service or costs, consider transferring.

■ **The little things:** We're talking pens, printer cartridges, tea bags, cleaning products, etc. Do you buy your office supplies on the high street as and when you need them? If so, consider wholesalers and buying in bulk; it could save you hundreds of pounds over the year.

Increasing productivity

Managing your time effectively will help you to be more productive. This means you can get more done for your customers, make time for your team and most importantly, get through your to-do list so it doesn't become a burden of unfinished tasks.

You should find time on a Friday to plan your week ahead. If you're at your best first thing in the morning, devote that time to business development tasks such as sales calls or product launches, the afternoon to strategy planning and high-level thinking, and the rest of the day to operational tasks like supplier meetings, invoice payments or team appraisals.

If you're more of a night owl, do your sales preparation when you have the most energy – but not late at night; a sales introduction email to a new client at 11 p.m. doesn't look professional. Try and stick to business hours or set up the email to go the next morning.

Think about when you have meetings outside of the office; if possible, aim to have all your meetings on the same day so that during the rest of the week you can have time in the office without having to leave. If this isn't possible, schedule the mornings or the end of the day for being out and about.

Emails and social media can be a distraction during the working day, so try to schedule time in the morning and late afternoon to tackle your inbox and connect online, leaving you free to get on with the most important tasks for most of the day.

Another way to increase productivity is to prioritize your to-do list. To distinguish what is a priority from what is not, think in terms of what will really drive your business forward versus the nuts-and-bolts operations that are part and parcel of running your business. As a start-up, you'll always have to get your hands dirty, but by dealing with your priorities, you'll end the week feeling like you've accomplished something tangible, which will keep you motivated and enthusiastic in the long term. Making a sales pitch or spending time talking to customers will always be more beneficial to your long-term business success than tidying the stock room. However, certain everyday tasks, such as making sure your invoices are paid on time, should always sit high on your list.

On a Monday morning put a calendar alert in your diary that reminds you to ask yourself the question: *Is it a priority?* Then go through your to-do list asking this question and marking each item on the list with one of the following statements.

- Yes, I must do it.
- Yes, but I can delegate it.
- Not right now, so I'll defer it.
- Not at all, so I'll ditch it.

When you get to the end of your list, you'll see clearly what you can cross off, what you need to get help with, and what you can do when you have more time available.

Managing failure

Starting and running a business is a courageous thing to do and requires passion and enthusiasm, but don't let your feelings blind you to the areas where your business isn't actually working. If you're finding your days are filled with tasks but you're not actually making any money and you're at risk of losing all of your savings and investment, or not being able to pay the mortgage, think seriously about whether or not you've got your business model right.

Go back to your business plan (Step 2). Were your assumptions about your customers proved right? Have you managed to win new work and recurring custom? Are your products costed correctly? If you can't answer these questions positively, take action to fix things. Talk to your accountant, to your mentor or any available business advisors and discuss your options, which might include winding up the company, selling part or all of the company, seeking an experienced business partner or diversifying your offering. Come up with a plan of action now. Your business is too important for you to bury your head in the sand in the hope that things will all miraculously fix themselves. They won't.

Try to remain upbeat about your future and believe in what you're doing. No matter what happens, or whether the business succeeds or not, you'll have learnt a great deal, developed new skills and created a new network of friends and colleagues.

Don't be embarrassed about getting it wrong – or by the f-word: failure. Some of the world's greatest entrepreneurs, James Dyson, Donald Trump, Bill Gates and Anita Roddick had multiple failures before they hit the big time. Think of it as earning your business stripes!

Developing support systems

Your relationship with a mentor or coach is a personal one but it's also a business transaction (even if it's free), so if it isn't working, don't be afraid to terminate it and find someone else.

Finding a mentor

Generally, a mentor will be another business person who knows your industry or has specific business skills that you admire. They will be willing to share their expertise, experiences and wisdom. Think about what you need and want from a mentor. For example, mentors could be:

■ inspirational people, for example, a successful person or a great speaker.

■ people with specific business expertise, for example, a great sales person.

■ people with relevant industry sector experience.

■ people who can offer peer support and act as a sounding board; being an entrepreneur can be lonely and it's refreshing to talk to someone who can provide encouragement whilst understanding what can realistically be achieved.

■ people who have a work or life situation that is similar to yours. For example, if you're a single mother, your mentor might be a woman in the same personal situation.

Mentors can also ask you challenging questions and hold you to account. It's harder to give up on something when you know that someone will be questioning you as to why you've done so.

Mentoring might involve regular phone calls, meetings or email exchanges, or could be carried out over dinner or coffee. Much will depend on your mentor's availability and meetings will often be on their terms. You may decide to approach someone you already know and respect to ask if they'll mentor you. However informal the relationship, it's beneficial to agree the terms upfront so that you both know what to expect. This can be done verbally or in writing. And remember: keep your aims SMART (see Step 5). Specifics that should be covered in any agreement include:

- short-term and long-term goals and aims that you want to achieve from the mentoring.

- the duration of the mentoring relationship.

- when and where meetings will take place.

- who will arrange the meeting places.

- how long meetings will last.

- whether the mentor can be contacted between meetings.

- who will pick up the bill if you meet over meals or drinks.

If you don't know anyone who would be right for the mentoring you need, there are formal mentoring services available, some of which are free and some of which charge a fee, where your needs can be matched with an appropriate and experienced mentor, who usually gives their time on a voluntary basis. Try the following websites.

www.mentorsme.co.uk

www.rockstargroup.co.uk

www.ukbusinessmentoring.co.uk

It might also be worth checking with your bank or other investors to see if they offer mentoring as an additional service.

Sounding Pro

Approaching a mentor for the first time can be daunting. Always avoid the direct question: 'Will you be my mentor?' as it tends to put people on the spot, asking them for a commitment they might not be ready to give, especially if they have only just met you. Then if you're lucky enough to secure a good mentor, it is essential to maintain the relationship.

Making the first approach
Hello (Raj), I'm (Ellen Walton). I was inspired by your talk today and everything you've achieved with your business. I, too, started a business this year. I realize that you're a busy man but I wondered if you could spare the time for a chat over a cup of coffee. I'd really appreciate your opinion and guidance.

Keeping the relationship going
Thank you for your time today, (Raj). I really value your opinion and your mentorship on this issue. You've helped me to see things in a different way and I'd really like to discuss progress and further challenges with you. Would you be willing to meet up again next month to follow up on our discussion?

Showing your appreciation, constantly
Thank you for agreeing to meet with me again today, (Raj). The advice you gave me in our last meeting has been invaluable. Let me share with you where I've got to since then.

If there's anything that I can help you with, or if you'd like to bounce ideas off me, please feel free.

Finding a business coach

A coach is a trained and qualified individual who provides their services as a formal business transaction. Coaches use industry standard tools, techniques and questioning to help you to identify your goals and develop an action plan to achieve them. They're not usually industry experts themselves and will rarely give you specific advice. Their value is in helping you to reach your goals faster than you would alone. However, you may decide to approach both a coach and a mentor.

If you decide to try coaching, you may start to find that there's some overlap between business and personal coaching. This is no real surprise; as a business owner, your business is a big part of your life, and your personal motivations, fears and circumstances will often affect how you approach your business. It's worth discussing this with your coach upfront and agreeing what areas your coaching sessions will cover.

A good coach can help you to progress rapidly towards your goals and will help you to question why you've chosen specific goals and whether they're still valid for you. They'll question your motivations and help you to understand what drives you as an individual (e.g. money, family, desire for control or credibility) so that you can use this knowledge to help shape your goals.

Coaching can be done face to face, online or over the telephone. Try a few different methods to begin with to see what suits you best. Face to face is useful because it helps the coach to see your body language and other non-verbal communication, but online and telephone coaching can save you travel time and therefore be more efficient and often cheaper.

Coaching has become a booming business and there are literally thousands of coaches to choose from, so it's worth seeking out referrals or recommendations from contacts or other business owners within your network before selecting one. Otherwise, try a local business network as they may be able to recommend a few coaches in the local area. Choose one that has experience or qualifications in the areas that you're looking for help with. And don't be afraid to question them – most will provide a free intake session or call during which you'll have the opportunity to do this. Ask for references and make sure you check them out thoroughly.

Your coach will usually provide a contract and submit invoices for their services. They may ask you to sign up for a number of sessions, often six or eight initially, as it usually takes a while for you to get to where you want to be and achieve your goals. The cost of coaching can vary immensely, anything from around £50 per hour to hundreds of pounds for some of the most respected and well-known coaches.

Self-coaching

Whether you've decided to engage the services of a coach or mentor or not, it's worth considering self-coaching to help you to remain motivated and proactive in reaching your goals. This doesn't have to be complicated; it simply involves taking control of your actions and formulating a plan. Use the following process.

- ■ Make a list of your goals, along with your hopes and challenges. Be sure to write them down.

- ■ Next, begin to prioritize the list. It's likely that some items will overlap and you'll have included short-, medium- and long-term goals.

- ■ Now write down a list of actions that you need to take to achieve each goal. If in some cases you're unsure of exactly what needs doing, think about what help you need and where you might find it.

- ■ Put deadlines against each action, along with review dates and what you'll do to celebrate when you've achieved each goal.

- ■ Add the actions to any existing to-do lists.

- ■ Lastly, review your hopes and challenges to see if any of your new actions will help with those too. If not, create a new set of actions which address these.

There are books, tools and articles available to help you with self-coaching should you wish to delve further into this technique. Search the internet to see what's available.

Looking after yourself

Getting a business off the ground takes a lot of hard work. In the first few months it's important not to forget about keeping yourself fit, healthy and happy. After all, where will the business be without its leader? It's all too easy to become absorbed in your passion but you also want to be fighting fit once everything is up and running so that you're able to enjoy it.

Remember to congratulate yourself and celebrate key milestones and little successes with family and friends. They've probably been seeing a lot less of you since you started your business, so it's important to schedule in quality time with them and discuss what you've been working on and how it's all going. This will help them to understand things better.

And don't forget to relax as often as you can! Take a deep breath and do something relaxing. Yes, getting a business off the ground is hard work and can be very stressful. There's no denying that you need to put the hours in, especially if you're trying to start up a new business while holding down a nine-to-five job, but don't do it to the detriment of your health. Keep up those sporting pursuits; aside from keeping you fit, they're a great way of de-stressing and letting off steam.

Giving back

There is a growing trend toward businesses acting in a socially and environmentally responsible way. For some businesses, this involves thinking about how to use less packaging on food products, which not only saves money but also helps reduce waste that ends up in landfills. For others, it might involve working with a local school to provide work experience opportunities to students. Thinking about how your business gives back is something that will set you apart from your competition in the long term and is a more strategic way of thinking about marketing your business to clients and consumers. If you're pitching for government contracts, for example, you might be asked to highlight your environmental policy or possible community involvement. The great thing is that thinking this way not only impacts your bottom line but you also benefit the environment or local community at the same time.

Key take-aways

Think about the things you will take away from Step 7 and how you will implement them.

Topic	Take-away	Implementation
The importance of taking stock	• It's important to review all aspects of my business at regular intervals if it is to remain efficient and improve. • Understanding what's worked and what hasn't worked is very important.	• Review progress against my business plan annually. • Make lists of successes and failures against each part of the business plan and develop an action plan accordingly.
Reviewing business performance		
Understanding the culture of my business		
Assessing the effectiveness of my networks		
Reviewing expenditure		
Increasing productivity		
Becoming a good leader		
Finding a mentor		
Finding a business coach		
Developing self-coaching techniques		
Looking after number one		
Giving back		